Studies in Language Sciences

Journal of the Japanese Society for Language Sciences

Volumes 16 & 17, March 2018

Editors

Kaoru Horie, Nagoya University
Takaaki Suzuki, Kyoto Sangyo University
Wataru Suzuki, Miyagi University of Education

Associate Editors

Yuko Goto Butler, University of Pennsylvania
Kazuhiko Fukushima, Kansai Gaidai University
Eric Hauser, University of Electro-Communication
Makiko Hirakawa, Chuo University
Shunji Inagaki, Doshisha University
Kuniyoshi Kataoka, Aichi University
Harumi Kobayashi, Tokyo Denki University
Tomoko Matsui, Tokyo Gakugei University
Junko Mori, University of Wisconsin-Madison
Kei Nakamura, Meikai University
Mineharu Nakayama, Ohio State University
Tsuyoshi Ono, University of Alberta
Miyuki Sasaki, Nagoya City University
Yasuhiro Shirai, Case Western Reserve University
Satoko Suzuki, Macalester College
Katsuo Tamaoka, Nagoya University
Timothy Vance, Komatsu University
Kei Yoshimoto, Tohoku University

Editorial Advisory Board

Niko Besnier, University of Amsterdam
Jack Bilmes, University of Hawai'i at Mānoa
Bernard Comrie, University of California, Santa Barbara
Fred Genesee, McGill University
Roberta Golinkoff, University of Delaware
Brian MacWhinney, Carnegie Mellon University
James McClelland, Stanford University
Andrea Moro, San Raffaele
William O'Grady, University of Hawai'i at Mānoa
Yuriko Oshima-Takane, McGill University
Yukio Otsu, Meikai University
Andrew Radford, University of Essex
Bonnie Schwartz, University of Hawai'i at Mānoa
Dan Slobin, University of California, Berkeley
Catherine Snow, Harvard University
Michael Tomasello, Duke University

Editorial Assistant

Nathan Hamlitsch, Mie University

Copyright © the Japanese Society for Language Sciences 2018

Kaitakusha Co., Ltd.
5-2, Mukogaoka 1-chome, Bunkyo-ku, Tokyo 113-0023
Japan

All rights reserved. No part of this publication may be reproduced, stored in a retrieval system, or transmitted, in any form or by any means, electronic, mechanical, photocopying, recording, or otherwise, without the prior permission of the copyright owner.

First published 2018

Published in Japan by Kaitakusha Co., Ltd.

Cover design by Shihoko Nakamura

Contents

Notes from the Editors iv
    Kaoru HORIE, Takaaki SUZUKI, and Wataru SUZUKI

List of Contributors vi

I. Linguistics

Interpretability of noun-modifying constructions in Japanese 1
    Paul GANIR

II. First Language Acquisition

Children's syntactic positional knowledge of a quantifier in Japanese 32
    Emi CALEY-KOMINE

北京在住日中国際結婚家庭の言語使用に関する一考察：
家庭言語政策の枠組みを用いて 44
    柳瀬千惠美

III. Second Language Acquisition

Deictic expressions in L2 narratives in Japanese: The case of
demonstratives and donatory verbs 66
    Noriko YABUKI-SOH

Verbal short-term memory's phonological features in first- to
seventh-grade Japanese EFL students 92
    Yasuyuki SAKUMA

文法指導の順序に関する実証的研究：中国語の動詞接辞"了1"と
文末助詞"了2"に焦点を当てて 117
    許　挺傑・鈴木祐一・劉　驫

Notes from the Editors

This is the sixteenth-seventeenth combined volume of *Studies in Language Sciences*, a publication of the Japanese Society for Language Sciences (JSLS, http://www.jsls.jpn.org/). The volume consists of selected papers that were originally presented at the annual JSLS conferences as well as general submission papers that were not presented at our annual conference.

JSLS was born from a first language acquisition community in Japan, and it now covers a wide range of language-related fields such as first and second language acquisition, linguistics, psychology, education, speech communication, computational models of language learning/processing, discourse and conversation analysis, and neurolinguistics. By promoting interdisciplinary research incorporating various approaches in language sciences, we hope to increase our knowledge of human language and the cognitive processes underlying it, and apply the knowledge to such practical matters as language teaching and software development.

To achieve this goal, we try to make our annual conference truly international. Most existing Japanese academic conferences in the area of language sciences appear to be functioning as a forum for domestic researchers to present their own work, and to learn from invited speakers from overseas. This is important, of course, but we JSLS treat our annual conference as an international forum to present and discuss research on language sciences, and we strive for a society that ensures two-way exchange of ideas between Japanese researchers and international communities of scientists.

This goal has been achieved to some extent in the first 10 years. For example, in 2008, approximately 40% of abstracts were from overseas, both in terms of nationality and affiliation of the presenters, which included countries such as the USA, China, Taiwan, Korea, Germany, and Canada. In addition, the number of abstracts submitted for presentation in English was twice that for presentation in Japanese. To ensure the international nature of our conference, JSLS maintains an English-Japanese bilingual policy, and has made every effort to make sure its activities will be useful for members and participants who do not know Japanese. One such endeavor is the selected proceedings of our annual conference *Studies in Language Sciences*, which had been published in English (with Japanese abstracts) from Kurosio Publishers. In our review process, we invite top experts in the subfields of language sciences both from Japan and abroad to ensure high quality of the published papers. However, this practice had not met the needs of members who want to publish their research in Japanese. Starting with the SLS 11, we started publishing papers written in Japanese as well to further uphold our bilingual policy. At the same time, we have changed the format of our publication from an edited volume to a refereed journal (*Studies in Language Sciences: the*

Journal of the Japanese Society for Language Sciences).

The change of format from edited volume to a journal necessitated changes in our editorial system. We now have three editors, 18 associate editors, and 16 editorial advisory board members. Our primary goal in editing *Studies in Language Sciences*, as with the previous volumes, is to select and publish work of the highest quality. In accordance with standard procedures for most international refereed journals, our editorial policy employed double-blind reviews by outside experts in the authors' fields of inquiry so that all the work published will meet the standard of each discipline. The selection of the reviewers was in accordance with one of the main objectives of the JSLS: to establish a truly international English and Japanese bilingual forum. We certainly could not have completed this volume without their contribution. We would like to thank the following individuals for their extensive and thoughtful reviews:

Yuka Akiyama (University of Tokyo)
Isao Iori (Hitotsubashi University)
Naomi H. McGloin (University of Wisconsin-Madison)
Satomi Mori (Rikkyo University)
Yuko Nakahama (Keio University)
Janice Nakamura (Sagami Women's University)
Hiroshi Nakanishi (Tohoku Gakuin University)
Hiromi Ozeki (Reitaku University)
Shogo Sakurai (Nanyang Technological University)
Neal Snape (Gunma Prefectural Women's University)
Yi-ching Su (National Tsing Hua University)
Kosuke Sugai (Kindai University)
Koji Sugisaki (Kwansei Gakuin University)
Ryoko Suzuki (Keio University)
Akiko Takahashi (Miyagi University of Education)
Yumi Takamiya (University of Alabama at Birmingham)
Miwa Takeuchi (University of Calgary)
Mari Umeda (Gunma Prefectural Women's University)
Fumio Watanabe (Yamagata University)
Foong Ha Yap (The Chinese University of Hong Kong, Shenzen)

Finally, we are most grateful to Masaru Kawata of Kaitakusha and Nathan Hamlitsch of Mie University, for their efficient and dedicated support in the preparation of this volume.

Kaoru Horie
Takaaki Suzuki
Wataru Suzuki
Editors, *Studies in Language Sciences*

List of Contributors

Caley-Komine, Emi
Department of English
Meiji Gakuin University
1-2-37 Shirokanedai, Minato-ku
Tokyo, 108-8636 Japan
E-mail: emi.mg@nifty.com

Liu, Biao
Faculty of Languages and Cultures
Kyushu University
744 Motooka Nishi-ku,
Fukuoka City, 819-0395 Japan
E-mail: liu@flc.kyushu-u.ac.jp

Ganir, Paul
Ph.D. Student, Department of East Asian Languages and Cultures
Stanford University
521 Memorial Way
Stanford, CA, 94305 USA
E-mail: pganir@stanford.edu

Sakuma, Yasuyuki
Faculty of Human Development and Culture
Fukushima University
1 Kanayagawa, Fukushima-shi,
Fukushima Prefecture, 960-1296 Japan
E-mail: ysakuma@educ.fukushima-u.ac.jp

Suzuki, Yuichi
The Department of Cross Cultural Studies
Kanagawa University
3-27-1 Rokkakubashi Kanagawa-ku,
Yokohama, 221-8686 Japan
E-mail: szky819@kanagawa-u.ac.jp

Xu, Tingjie
Department of Global Studies
Oita Prefectural College of Arts and Culture
1-11, Uenogaoka Higashi, Oita city,
Oita, 870-0833 Japan
E-mail: kyo@oita-pjc.ac.jp

Yabuki-Soh, Noriko
Department of Languages, Literatures and Linguistics
York University
4700 Keele Street, Ross South 561,
Toronto, Ontario, M3J 1P3 Canada
E-mail: nyabuki@yorku.ca

Yanase, Chiemi
Graduate School of Social and Cultural Studies
Kyushu University
744 Motooka, Nishi-ku, Fukuoka,
Fukuoka, 819-0395 Japan
E-mail: chinta1959@yahoo.co.jp

Interpretability of noun-modifying constructions in Japanese

Paul GANIR, Stanford University

Abstract

The Japanese noun-modifying construction can express a variety of meanings such as a relative clause or a noun complement clause despite having one general structure. Previous frameworks grounded in syntax, semantics, and pragmatics have analyzed how such meanings can be derived from one structure (e.g. Keenan & Comrie, 1977; Comrie, 1996, 1998; Matsumoto, 1988, 1997, 2007). This paper expands on existing analyses by using empirical survey data to shed light on how syntactic, semantic, and pragmatic information contribute to a successful construal of Japanese noun-modifying constructions. Based on interpretability ratings of 30 experimental items, participants used an aggregate of syntactic, semantic, and pragmatic information to reach a construal. The results suggest that, in the case of Japanese, successful interpretation of noun-modifying constructions relies more on word choice and being able to derive a plausible relationship between the modifying clause and the head noun. From a typological perspective, this study casts doubt on whether the concept of a "relative clause" is applicable for cross-linguistic comparisons.

1. Introduction

Ranging from relative clauses to noun complements and more, Japanese noun-modifying constructions (NMCs) have provided a rich source of data and discussion about how people derive interpretability. Beginning with Keenan and Comrie's (1977) typological discussion of relative clauses, Japanese constructions have been treated using a syntax-driven approach. However, work by Matsumoto (e.g. 1988, 1997) has argued for the need to include semantics and pragmatics in interpreting the range of Japanese constructions. As these analyses generally have been qualitative, this paper supplies empirical evidence to better understand the processes involved in deriving an interpretation.

This paper begins by providing preliminary information about the structure of Japanese and Japanese NMCs. Next, it reviews the different approaches to analyzing Japanese NMCs to highlight the interaction of factors determining interpretability. The paper then investigates this interaction through a survey experiment and presents that data. From those empirical results I argue that successful interpretation of constructions like Japanese NMCs can be interpreted syntactically but are more dependent on semantic and pragmatic word associations.

2. Literature review
2.1. Structure of Japanese and its noun-modifying constructions

Typologically, Japanese is classified as a verb-final language (e.g. Iwasaki, 2013; Martin, 1975). Constituents are marked with postpositional case particles, such as the nominative *ga*, accusative *o*, and dative *ni*, to indicate their relationship to the predicate, although these particles may often be omitted, especially during conversation. As an SOV language, Japanese sentences are commonly ordered as subject-object-verb for transitive verbs and subject-indirect object-direct object-verb for ditransitive verbs. However, permutation of constituents is allowed; this can be seen in the examples (1) and (2)[1]:

(1) *ringo-wa*   *hanako-ga*   *inu-ni*   *yatta.*
    apple-TOP   (name)-NOM   dog-DAT   give:PAST
    'The apple, Hanako gave it to the dog.'

(2) *inu-ni-wa*   *hanako-ga*   *ringo-o*   *yatta.*
    dog-DAT-TOP   (name)-NOM   apple-ACC   give:PAST
    'To the dog, Hanako gave an apple.'
    (Iwasaki, 2013, p. 13)

Additionally, as with case particles, Japanese allows for the elision of arguments, especially when information can be retrieved from context. A conversation such as (3) illustrates the ellipsis of subject and direct object:

(3) A: *mita*   *no?*   'Have (you) seen (it)?'
         see:PAST   SE
    B: *mita*   *yo.*   '(I)'ve seen (it).'
         see:PAST   PP
         (Iwasaki, 2013, p. 13)

Given these preliminaries, let us now turn to noun-modifying constructions (NMCs) in Japanese. As Matsumoto (2007, 2010, 2017) observes, NMCs are constructions formed by a noun or noun phrase modified by an adnominal clause in a finite form, shown in (4):

(4) [[Predicate (finite/prenominal form)] Noun]

---

[1] The abbreviations used are as follows: ABL: ablative, ACC: accusative, ASP: aspect, COMP: complementizer, DAT: dative, FAM.DIM: familiar diminutive, GOAL: goal, HON: honorific, INSTR: instrument, LOC: locative, NOM: nominative, NONPAST: non-past, PASS: passive, PAST: past, POL: polite, PP: pragmatic particle, QP: question particle, SE: sentence extender, TE: *-te* (conjunctive), TOP: topic marking particle.

As Matsumoto (2017) notes, the predicate is the essential member of this construction, with the modifying-clause predicate being in the adnominal form, with the exception of nominal adjectives in the non-past form (e.g. the nominal adjective *kiree* 'pretty' in its adnominal form would be *kireena* as opposed to finite *kireeda*). While having one general structure, this schematic covers a range of constructions. One function is to form "relative clause" constructions, where the head noun is relativized from the predicate. Sentences (5) – (8) represent such constructions. As the sentences illustrate, the symbol ∅ denotes the original location of the head noun. In (5), the relativized *kimura-san* 'Mr. Kimura' functions as the subject of the relative clause; the non-relative equivalent is given in the parenthesis below it. Similarly, the head noun *inu* 'dog' in (6) is coreferential with the direct object of the relative clause, *kodomo* 'child' in (7) the indirect object, and *kuruma* 'car' in (8) the instrument. In such cases, the relationship between the "relative clause" and the head noun is straightforward. That is, one can reconstruct the unrelativized version by taking the head noun, reinserting it into the "gap" in the relative clause with the appropriate case particle.

(5) Subject relative
[∅   inu   o   katte-iru]
      dog   ACC keep:TE-ASP:NONPAST
Kimura-san
(name)-Mr.
'Mr. Kimura, who has a dog'
(cf. *kimura-san ga inu o katte-iru*)

(6) Direct object relative
[*Kimura-san*   ga   ∅   katte-iru]
(name)-Mr.   NOM   keep:TE-ASP:NONPAST
inu
dog
'the dog that Mr. Kimura has'
(cf. *kimura-san ga sono inu o katte-iru*)

(7) Indirect object relative
[*Kimura-san*   ga   ∅   inu   o   ageta]
(name)-Mr.   NOM   dog   ACC gave
kodomo
child
'the child to whom Mr. Kimura gave a dog'
(cf. *kimura-san ga sono kodomo ni inu o ageta*)
(Iwasaki, 2013, p. 202)

(8) [*Taroo*   ga   ∅   kaisya   e   iku]
(name)   NOM   company   GOAL go

> *kuruma*
> car
> 'the car by which Taroo goes to his company'
> (cf. *taroo ga kuruma de kaisya e iku*)
> (Matsumoto, 1988, p. 166)

However, Japanese NMCs also occur in ways where the head noun does not appear to have a "gapped" relation in the modifying clause. Sentence (9) is an example of such a construction. As the parenthetical equivalent shows, it is possible to phrase the sentence without an NMC by using an adverbial clause.

> (9) [*atama   ga   yokunaru*]   *hon*
>   head   NOM   improve   book
> 'the book (by reading) which (one's) head improves
> (cf. *kono hon o yomeba atama ga yokunaru* 'if (one) reads this book, (one's) head improves)
> (Matsumoto, 1988, p. 167)

Japanese NMCs can also be seen in constructions where the head nouns can be understood as providing a label for the preceding content (Iwasaki, 2013) or a frame for hosting the information expressed by the modifying clause (Matsumoto, 1997). Some of these nouns include words of speech, thought, states, perception, and relational concepts. The perception head noun *nioi* 'smell' in (10) is one example, where information about the 'smell' — namely, its origin — is provided in the modifying clause *sakana o yaku* 'to grill fish'.

> (10) [*sakana o   yaku*]   *nioi*
>   fish   ACC   grill   smell
> 'the smell (of) grilling fish'
> (Matsumoto, 1988, p. 173)

Another function of this construction is to convey noun complement clauses, as in (11):

> (11) [*tikyuu   ga   marui*]   *zizitu*
>   earth   NOM   round   fact
> 'the fact that the earth is round'
> (Matsumoto, 1997, p. 1)

As a consequence of the range of meanings expressed by this one form, this construction has been noted to cover a wide, if not the widest, range of meanings that are often conveyed by different structures in other languages such as relative clause constructions, noun complement constructions, and those expressed by gerunds and adjectives (Matsumoto, 1988, 1997; Wang, Horie, & Pardeshi, 2009).

2.2. Typological considerations and analyses of Japanese NMCs

Typologically, Japanese NMCs have been examined from their function as a relative clause construction. In Keenan and Comrie's (1977) work over 50 languages, they posited a universal Accessibility Hierarchy where languages, including Japanese, relativize noun phrases in a specific hierarchy. They argue that this hierarchy, shown in (12), not only predicts the variety of relativization strategies in languages but also reflects the psychological ease of comprehension; they claim that constructions with noun phrases lower on the hierarchy are more difficult to understand than constructions with noun phrases higher on the continuum.

(12) Accessibility Hierarchy
SU > DO > IO > OBL > GEN > OCOMP
(SU = subject; DO = direct object; IO = indirect object; OBL = major oblique case; GEN = genitive; OCOMP = object of comparison)

Studies on language processing and first language acquisition focus on children's acquisition of relative clauses in English, with particular focus on SU and DO relatives (e.g. Brown, 1971; Sheldon, 1974; de Villiers et al., 1979; Tavakolian, 1981; Kidd & Bavin, 2002). With English-speaking children, studies like de Villiers et al. (1979), Diessel and Tomasello (2000), and Diessel and Tomasello (2005) found that children appear to acquire SU relatives earlier than DO and OBL relatives and that children have fewer errors in SU relatives compared to DO and OBL relatives. This evidence suggests that the Accessibility Hierarchy can be used to predict the acquisition order or relative clauses. On the other hand, studies on other languages have found contrasting results. Of note are Ozeki and Shirai (2007) and Yip and Matthews (2007). Ozeki and Shirai (2007) analyzed conversational data from Japanese children and found that they acquired and used SU, DO, and OBL relatives at around the same rate. Yip and Matthews (2007) examined the grammatical development of Hong Kong Cantonese-English bilingual children and found that DO relatives emerged earlier or at the same time as SU relatives. These findings in Japanese and Cantonese challenge the notion of the Accessibility Hierarchy as a linguistic universal.

In light of cross-linguistic research on relative clause constructions, Comrie (1996, 1998, 2002) suggests a different typology, categorizing languages as either adhering to a "European" type or an "Asian" type. This distinction is based on analyses using the syntactic ideas of extraction or accessibility. For instance, English, which falls under the "European" type, relativizes nouns by extracting them from the modifying clause and uses a relative pronoun to indicate its relation to the clause. This can be illustrated in (13) and (14), where *whom* indicates the case of the extracted direct object *man* from the direct object position (represented by the -):

(13) I saw the man
(14) the man [whom [I saw -]]
    (Comrie, 1998, p. 64)

Japanese, however, cannot be analyzed using the same approach. At first glance, it appears to apply, as seen in (15) and (16):

(15) *gakusei ga   hon   o   katta.*
     student NOM   book   ACC   bought
     'The student bought the book.'
(16) [*gakusei   ga   katta*]   *hon*
     student   NOM   bought   book
     'the book [that the student bought -]'
     (Matsumoto, 1997, p. 4)

Unlike a language like English, however, and as noted in the previous section, Japanese allows for omission of predicate arguments while still being grammatical. (17), being an acceptable sentence, is an example of a construction that disputes the notion of gaps as an applicable analysis to Japanese "relative clauses":

(17) *gakusei ga   katta.*
     student NOM   bought
     'The student bought (it).'

Testing the idea of extraction on other Japanese constructions which follow the *modifying clause + head noun* structure, such as fact-S constructions like 'the fact [that the student bought the book]', Comrie concluded that Japanese falls under an "Asian" typology which cannot be adequately explained using conventional syntactic analyses.

In contrast to syntax-focused analyses, Matsumoto (1988, 1997) offers an analysis which highlights the importance of semantic and pragmatic factors. This approach provides several advantages over previous analyses. First, while syntactic accounts can explain some Japanese NMCs that can be interpreted as relative clauses, it does not account for the range of NMCs and the variety of semantic relationships represented between the modifying clause-head and the noun. For instance, while Keenan and Comrie's Accessibility Hierarchy describes a continuum of relationships between head nouns and the modifying clause, this is only relevant to the constructions that can be interpreted as relative clauses. Since relative clauses are only one subset of Japanese NMCs, Matsumoto argues that the successful interpretation of other meanings expressed with this construction, such as Examples (9) – (11), uses strategies not based on syntax alone but also uses semantic and pragmatic mechanisms.

Second, recall that Japanese allows for the omission of arguments. This omission, in conjunction with the absence of a relative pronoun, may allow for multiple interpretations of a single NMC, such as in (18):

(18) [[*yonde-iru*] *kodomo*] *wa doko desu ka.*
 calling-is child TOP where is QP
 'Where is the child (who) is calling (someone)?' OR
 'Where is the child (whom) (someone) is calling?'
 (Matsumoto, 1997, p. 39)

While such ambiguity can occur, Matsumoto remarks that arriving on an interpretation requires the application of extra-linguistic factors such as context and real-world knowledge.

3. Interpreting Japanese NMCs

The current literature presents Japanese NMCs as a rich set of constructions that are interpreted using a combination of syntactic, semantic, and pragmatic information. If in cases where Japanese NMCs can be interpreted as relative clauses and thus primarily use syntactic information, people should be able to say whether or not those NMCs are interpretable, regardless of real-world silliness. That is, given a construction like *tookyoo o tabeta tomato* 'the tomato (which) ate Tokyo (Matsumoto, 1997, p. 83), people should be able to say that the construction is interpretable, despite the implausibility of a tomato eating Tokyo. Consequently, given the predictions made in Keenan and Comrie's Accessibility Hierarchy, if Japanese NMCs are understood as relative clauses, the difficulty of comprehending the constructions depends on the position of the relativized head nouns within the Hierarchy.

In cases where Japanese NMCs do not exhibit a syntactic gap, it is necessary to consider what other information is available in the construction to produce a possible construal. One such way is to consider the argument structure of the verbs in the modifying predicate. For instance, the argument structure for the verb *hit* can be expressed as having someone who performs the action and an object which receives the action, resulting in a two-argument construction. In this way, verbs prescribe what is necessary to form a well-formed, interpretable construction but not specifically other elements that could be part of the construction. Pustejovsky's (1995) description of the argument structure of lexical items, however, provides a richer distinction, shown in Table 1. Although Japanese NMCs allow for argument omission and can be formed without syntactic gaps, a framework like Pustejovsky's, which considers optional syntactic arguments as well as situational information, suggests that NMC interpretability may depend on knowledge beyond its structure.

Because Japanese can and often omits words and case markings in utterances, applying argument structure to Japanese may not always be neat. As (17) shows, the Japanese construction *gakusei ga katta* 'The student bought (it)' is a perfectly acceptable sentence; with context the construction *katta* '(I) bought (it)' would also be an ordinary construction. However, Japanese constructions still have their arguments. For instance, with an utterance like *gakusei ga katta*, *gakusei (ga)* 'student' is a True argument (the parenthesis clarifies the use of case markings) The utterance *taroo ga kuruma de kaisya e iku* 'Taro goes to his company by car' has *kuruma (de)* 'by car' as a Default argument. An utterance like *mearii ga kayoobi ni nyuuyooku ni iku* 'Mary will go to New York on Tuesday' has *kayoobi (ni)* 'on Tuesday' as a True adjunct.

Table 1. Pustejovsky's (1995) argument structure

Argument type	Description	Example
True argument	Syntactically realized parameters of the lexical item	*John arrived late*
Default argument	Parameters which participate in the logical expressions but are not necessarily expressed syntactically	*John built the house out of bricks*
Shadow argument	Parameters which are semantically incorporated into the lexical item; they can be expressed only by operations of subtyping or discourse specification	*Mary buttered her toast with an expensive butter*
True adjuncts	Parameters which modify the logical expression but are part of the situational interpretation and are not tied to any particular lexical item's semantic representation	*Mary drove down to New York on Tuesday*

In a similar vein, Fillmore's work on frame semantics (e.g. Fillmore, 1982; Fillmore & Atkins, 1992), derives language meaning not from any individual word but the scenes evoked by words. These scenes generate core and secondary lexical categories available in order to articulate the event. For instance, in a commercial transaction frame, one can identify the roles Buyer, Seller, Goods, and Money. Moreover, one can derive additional categories such as Cost, Tender, and Change.

Matsumoto (1997) applies this framework in her treatment of Japanese NMCs, and its usefulness can be seen in accounting for the relationships between modifying clauses and head nouns when no apparent syntactic gap can be seen. Matsumoto also emphasizes the importance of world-view knowledge, or "the organization of expectations that the participants of a discourse have from their individual past experience in certain cultures and societies or from the context of the specific discourse" (p. 74). That is, prior knowledge about the world influences the acceptability and interpretation of a construction. This particularly can be seen in constructions that invite multiple interpretations as in (19) and (20). In these sentences, the NMCs are identical except for two characters, *Tomo-tyan* and *Donarudo Toranpu*. With the former character denoting a young child and the latter a real estate developer, however, the two constructions lead to two structurally different interpretations.

(19) [[*Tomo-tyan*   *ga*   *katta*]   *mise*]   *wa*
      Tomo-FAM.DIM   NOM   bought   store   TOP
      doko.
      where
      'Where is the store (in which) little Tomo bought (   )?'

(20) [[*Donarudo*   *Toranpu*   *ga*   *katta*]   *mise*]
      Donald   Trump   NOM   bought   store
      wa   *doko*.
      TOP   where
      'Where is the store (which) Donald Trump bought?'

As these approaches differ in the way they conceptualize the meaning of constructions, their application to Japanese NMCs also have varying explanatory power. The syntactically-driven approach can explain the how NMCs may be interpreted when they function as relative clauses, but this limitation neglects NMCs which do not fall under that categorization. The argument structure approach can be applied to NMC construability primarily based on the arguments projected by the modifying clause's predicate, accounting for a broader range of NMCs and the kinds of relationships possible between modifying clauses and their head nouns. The frame-semantic approach has been shown to account for the variety of NMCs in Japanese by the relationships of the frames evoked by the modifying predicate and the head noun.

4. Present study

While the literature provides analyses of how various NMCs are interpreted, no study has empirically examined the rates of NMC interpretability in a controlled manner. Matsumoto (1997) provides an example of informal interviews asking participants to provide an interpretation for the construction *tookyoo o tabeta tomato* 'the tomato (which) ate Tokyo'. This study extends that interview idea by collecting survey data using a variety of NMCs, varying the head nouns while keeping modifying clauses unchanged, in order to shed more light on the process of interpretation and integration of information.

This study uses experimental items adapted from example sentences provided in previous studies (e.g. Matsumoto, 1997) with the aim of testing the applicability of the three approaches reviewed in the previous section. That is, the relationship between the head nouns and their modifying clauses can be explained as appearing to be "extracted" from various positions of the modifying clause, identified in Keenan and Comrie's Accessibility Hierarchy, corresponding to different types of arguments according to Pustejovsky, or occupying different frame-semantic roles depending on the frames evoked. Three conditions were chosen. In the first condition, or the Core Condition, head nouns were chosen such that they can be considered the syntactic subject, the only True argument or a core Agent role of the predicates. In the second condition, or the Oblique Condition, head nouns were chosen such that they were non-subjects, default or adjunct arguments, or non-core roles of the predicates. That is, relative to the predicates, these head nouns include information about roles or arguments of location, cause-effect, time, and instrument. In the third condition, or the Other Condition, head nouns were chosen such that they may be forced into a syntactic role of their modifying clauses but do not have a semantically or pragmatically clear relationship with them. An example of one base modifying clause with head nouns in the three conditions is given in Table 2. By combining the base modifying clause with the different head nouns, three experimental stimuli were constructed: *gohan o tabeta kookoosei* (Core Condition), *gohan o tabeta otyawan* (Oblique Condition), and *gohan o tabeta denki* (Other Condition). As previously described, each construction does not have an overt marker to indicate the relationship between the head noun and the modifying clause. However, the constructions were constructed to elicit an intended reading. In these particular cases, *kookoosei* 'high school student' is intended to elicit the subject or core Agent role, *otyawan* 'rice bowl' is intended to elicit a non-subject, non-core role as an instrument, and *denki* 'electric light' is intended to be a semantically and pragmatically unrelated word to the modifying clause.

Table 2. Noun-modifying clause stimuli item design

Base noun-modifying clause	Core Condition	Oblique Condition	Other Condition
ご飯 を 食べた *Gohan o tabeta* meal ACC ate	高校生 *kookoosei* high school student	お茶碗 *otyawan* rice bowl	電気 *denki* electric light

If the data were to follow the predictions given by Keenan and Comrie's (1977) Accessibility Hierarchy, participants are expected to rate items in the Core Condition as readily accessible, as the head nouns satisfy the subject position of the modifying predicate, the most accessible relativized position. Next, participants are expected to rate items in the Oblique Condition with moderate interpretability ratings, although not to the extent of the Core Condition. This is due to the head nouns being non-subjects, thus occupying a lower position on the Hierarchy. Finally, participants are expected to rate items in the Other Condition as interpretable, although perhaps not as high as the Core Condition and not as moderate as the Oblique Condition. The main reason for this prediction is that the head noun, despite having an unclear relationship with the modifying clause, presumably can be inserted into the "gap" in the modifying clause, therefore resulting in some kind of interpretable phrase. However, it is unclear how participants will try to relativize each head noun, so some variability is expected. For instance, in the construction *gohan o tabeta denki* 'the electric light ( ) ate a meal', it is possible to force a reading corresponding to the phrase 'the electric light which ate a meal.' The construction itself may make little sense, but it has no syntactic errors.

Similarly, if the data were to match with the principles of argument structure, one would expect that Core Condition items would be rated highly, Oblique Condition items mixed, and Other Condition items low. This is due to the obligatory expression of the head nouns as arguments of the modifying clause. In the Core Condition the head nouns function as True arguments and must be expressed, so its relationship to the predicate is highly recoverable. In the Oblique Condition, some of the head nouns fall under the categories of Default arguments or Adjuncts; their optional expression would be recoverable from the predicate, although presumably not as easily True arguments. However, some of the head nouns in this Condition are the content-taking type (e.g. *sakana o yaku nioi*, as in (10)). These content-taking nouns are not projected by the predicates but rather provide a label for the information in the modifying clause, so participants are expected to have trouble processing the construction and thus give lower construable ratings for them. In the Other Condition, the head nouns do not satisfy the arguments projected by the predicates, so participants may have difficulties interpreting them. Taking the construction *gohan o tabeta denki* 'the electric light ( ) ate a meal', the clause *gohan o tabeta* 'ate a meal' may project arguments such as the eater of the meal or an instrument for the meal, such as *kookoosei* 'high school student' or *otyawan* 'rice bowl', but the Other head noun *denki* 'electric light' is intended to not readily fill such arguments.

Lastly, if the data were to fit frame semantic approaches, participants are expected to give high ratings for items in Core and Oblique Conditions and low ratings for the Other Condition. The reasons for these ratings in the Core and Other Conditions follow a similar reasoning as in the argument structure approach, using the terminology of core or non-core roles evoked in frames rather than the arguments projected by predicates. However, unlike the argument structure approach, frame semantics predicts that as long as an appropriate frame can be understood from a given construction, the head noun should be easily interpreted as having some relationship with the modifying clause, whether it is a core role or a non-core role. These predictions are summarized in Table 3.

Table 3. Predicated participant ratings of NMCs based on framework

Framework	Predicted Participant Ratings		
	Core	Oblique	Other
Syntax	High	Moderate	Moderate to High
Argument Structure	High	Moderate to High	Low
Frame Semantics	High	High	Low

With Matsumoto's frame-semantic analysis explaining the variety of Japanese NMCs more neatly than other accounts, this study adopts her framework in hypothesizing that the interpretability of an NMC depends more on its semantics or pragmatics than syntax. As a consequence, this study makes the following predictions:

i) Because the relationship between the head noun and the modifying clause in Japanese NMCs are not explicitly marked, construability ratings of items in Core and Oblique Conditions should not differ significantly.

ii) If syntax is not the primary influence determining the construability of a Japanese NMC, participants will rate items in Other Condition as largely uninterpretable.

5. Experiment
5.1. Method
5.1.1. Participants

The study initially gathered 40 responses from native Japanese participants. Due to incomplete responses, 13 sets of responses were excluded for a final count of 27 participants. Of these 27 participants, 17 were male and 10 were female. Their ages ranged from 20 to over 60 years old, and their highest attained educational levels ranged from completion of high school to completion of a post-baccalaureate degree. Table 4 provides a breakdown of participants' demographic information.

Table 4. Participants' demographic information

Age (in years)	Number	%
< 20	0	0.0
20–29	7	25.9
30–39	6	22.2
40–49	5	18.5
50–59	3	11.1
>= 60	6	22.2
Total	**27**	**100.0**
Gender		
Male	17	62.9
Female	10	37.1
Total	**27**	**100.0**
Highest Educational Level Completed		
High School	3	11.1
Vocational/Technical School	6	22.2
Junior College	3	11.1
University	10	37.1
Graduate school	5	18.5
Total	**27**	**100.0**

5.1.2. Materials

Target constructions were constructed using the basic structure of Japanese noun-modifying constructions of [[Predicate (finite/prenominal form)] Noun]. First, ten base predicates were constructed. These base predicates were constructed such that they lacked only one true argument, namely the subject. These predicates were also constructed with consideration to other possible arguments or roles they may be project. For instance, take the predicate verb *taberu* 'to eat'. Since *taberu* projects the arguments of subject and direct object — or eater and food — the predicate was constructed so that an explicit direct object is given in the entire predicate, such as *gohan o tabeta* 'ate a meal'. However, *taberu* can also project arguments for eating utensils or location, which is taken under consideration when creating the head nouns for Oblique Condition (see below). As another example, the predicate *torusutoi o honyaku-sita* 'translated Tolstoy' projects a subject, but it may also allow for a head noun like *hoosyuu* 'payment', a consequence of the predicate. Continuing with the base predicates, head nouns were chosen to satisfy three conditions. As mentioned in the previous section, Core Condition head nouns can be understood as the syntactic subject, a true argument or a core Agent role of the predicates. Oblique Condition head nouns can be understood as non-subjects, default or adjunct arguments, or non-core roles of the predicates. Other Condition head nouns can be understood as having no semantically or pragmatically clear relationship with the predicates. Altogether, 30 experimental stimuli were constructed and were balanced with 30 filler constructions to distract participants from noticing patterns within the target experimental stimuli. All items were randomized into three blocks containing 10 target constructions and 10 fillers, and the three blocks were ordered randomly. A full list of the target and filler constructions is given in Appendices 1 and 2 (although English glosses are given, note they are only one possible interpretation). This study used a within-subjects design where each participant were exposed to and rated all 60 items. The study was designed using the Qualtrics Research Suite (Qualtrics, Provo, UT).

5.1.3. Procedure

Participants were given an online link to access the survey. After reading the survey consent form, participants were given the following directions:

> このアンケートは名詞節が解釈可能か不可能を調査することを目的とします。
> 設問は全部で60問です。
> 例文）　ちゃぶ台の上にあるラムネの空き瓶の色にも心を配る。
> 例文の下線を引いた部分である「ちゃぶ台の上にあるラムネの空き瓶」が設問の問題に出てきます。
> 切り抜いた言葉を見て、解釈が可能かどうかを「可能」か「不可能」でお答えください。

"This survey aims to investigate whether noun phrases are construable or not. There are 60 questions in total.
Example: '(He) also pays attention to the color of the empty lemonade bottle (which) was on the dining table.'
The questions will be given as in the underlined portion, "empty lemonade

bottle (which) was on the dining table".
Read the excerpted phrases and answer whether they are interpretable by selecting "Possible" or "Impossible".

The participants were then given an example item and given an additional instruction to answer using their intuition as there is a possibility that some excerpts might seem strange or unusual. Participants then judged 60 items for interpretability. Each question was presented separately, and participants were asked to judge whether it was possible or impossible to interpret. The rationale behind this choice was to see if participants had general tendencies to characterize the construability of noun-modifying constructions based on the semantic and pragmatic relationship between the modifying clause and the head noun.

At the end of the survey participants were asked to provide general demographic information. These questions included age, gender, occupation, and highest educational level reached. They were also free to leave comments about the survey.

5.2. Results

Figure 1 summarizes the participants' ratings over the three conditions on the basis of interpretability. Each item received 27 ratings of interpretability, and each condition contained a total of 270 ratings.

Participants' ratings for each item in Core, Oblique, and Other Conditions are given in Figures 2, 3, and 4. As Figure 2 indicates, participant responses over all 10 items in the Core Condition yielded an overall 96% rate of interpretability. Seven out of the 10 items received either a full 27/27 or a 26/27 rate of interpretability, and the lowest rated item was observed as interpretable by 24 participants. Figure 3 details participant responses for Oblique Condition items. Not unlike the Core Condition, participants rated items as highly interpretable, with an overall rate of about 88%. However, certain items were rated less interpretable, particularly items 1 (21/27, 78%) and 2 (13/27, 48%). These will be discussed in detail in the next section. Other Condition ratings present contrasting data to Core and Oblique, with each item being rated as mainly uninterpretable. Six of the 10 items were rated interpretable by less than 10% of the time, and four items — items 6, 8, 9, and 10 — were interpretable no more than 22% of the participants. The overall rate of interpretability was determined to be about 9%.

A mixed effects analysis of the relationship between participants' responses and conditions was conducted using the statistical program RStudio (R Core Team, 2015) and *lme4* (Bates, Maechler, Bolker, Walker, 2015). The model included condition as a fixed effect and participants and experimental items as random effects. Orthogonal contrasts were used to compare Core to Oblique and Core to Other. Results indicated that there was a significant difference in participant ratings between Core and Oblique ($\beta = -1.56$, $z = -6.61$, $p < 0.001$) as well as a significant difference between Core and Other ($\beta = 4.76$, $z = 12.61$, $p < 0.001$).

5.3. Discussion
5.3.1. Syntactic roles and semantic/pragmatic relationships

The data provide a strong indication that, while syntactic information may very well provide information to aid in interpretation, Japanese NMCs are construed with semantic and pragmatic primacy. As Matsumoto (1997) discussed, NMCs may give rise to multiple possible interpretations, and given little contextual background, interpretations where head nouns occupy a core role — oftentimes the subject of the predicate — are thought to be the most accessible. While this experiment focuses on whether a construction is, minimally, interpretable and not differentiating among possible interpretations, the participant ratings from Core and Oblique Conditions suggest that subject-occupying head nouns are easy to construe. These kinds of NMCs function similarly to relative clauses in other languages, and Keenan and Comrie's (1977) claim that relativized subjects are easiest to access is supported by the data.

However, turning to the ratings given in the Oblique Condition, constructions where the head nouns occupy a non-subject relation to the predicate received similar ratings to the items in the Core Condition. Although more data is needed to determine whether head nouns instantiating different syntactic roles can be ordered in a hierarchy, the results suggest that NMCs are generally interpretable as long as a reasonable relation can be inferred between the predicates and head nouns. For instance, the construction *torusutoi o honyaku-sita hoosyuu* 'the money (which) (resulted after) (someone) translated Tolstoy' has a modifying clause-head noun relation of Condition-Consequence (Matsumoto, 1997, p. 114), but this relation was reported to be construable by 23 out of 27 participants. This suggests that this kind of relationship, while easily interpretable, may not be as such when compared to constructions functioning as relative clauses. Even so, the corresponding item in the Core Condition, *torusutoi o honyaku-sita bungakusya* 'the literary scholar (who) translated Tolstoy', was rated as interpretable by 24 participants, or only one more participant, and so a relative clause account may not easily explain this minor difference. In both the Core Condition and Oblique Condition items, the relevant arguments/participants are expressed (e.g. the author Tolstoy and the scholar who translated (his work); the author Tolstoy and the payment for translation (of his work)), making the items interpretable.

Discrepancies regarding interpretability ratings and syntax can also be seen in the difference within the Oblique Condition items *gohan o tabeta otyawan* 'the rice bowl (someone used) to eat a meal' and *bataa o tokasita nabe* 'the saucepan (someone used) to melt butter'. In both items the head nouns *otyawan* 'rice bowl' and *nabe* 'sauce pan' were chosen with the intention of instantiating, according to the different frameworks, an oblique case, true argument, or an instrumental reading. However, despite the similarities in structure, the first example received an interpretable rating of 78% while the second example received a 100% rating. This is even more surprising considering that the former item is an attested item, although with a given context (Matsumoto, 1997). It is possible that the lack of a context made it difficult for some participants to reach an interpretation. Regardless of the actual cause, if participants understood these two constructions using a syntactic approach only, one would expect their ratings on these two items to be similar. The responses in the Other Condition also support the argument that NMC interpretability depends less on syntactic roles. While it is possible to create syntactically well-formed sentences using the same words without the use of the NMC structure, the fact that respondents indicated their uninterpretability suggests that they are uncertain how they would form a relationship with the modifying clauses and the head nouns to form meaningful sentences. This is supported further by the quantitative analysis using mixed effect models. While there was a significant difference between both Core and Oblique and Core and Other, the difference observed between Core and Oblique is small compared to the difference between Core and Other. At first glance, these results suggest that Core differs from both Oblique and Other. However, when considering the variance in participant judgments, it is found that the variance is less dependent on the syntax or argument structure and more on the semantic and pragmatic integrability of the modifying clauses and head nouns. That is, although Oblique items like *gohan o tabeta otyawan* 'the rice bowl (someone used) to eat a meal' and *tomato o tabeta nooen* 'the plantation (where) (someone) ate a tomato' that elicited low interpretability ratings and Other items like *kami o kitta zoo* 'the elephant (that) cut paper' were rated as interpretable by some participants, the overall ratings suggest that the items in the Other Condition were deemed uninterpretable due to having highly unrelated head nouns and modifying clauses.

It is interesting to note that in the Other Condition, animacy may factor in people's acceptability judgments. While most of the head nouns used in Other were inanimate objects, two constructions, *sakana o yaku ari* 'the ant (which) grills fish' and *kami o kitta zoo* 'the elephant (that) cut paper', have insects or animals as head nouns. This property of animacy can also be seen in Core Condition head nouns. All of the Core Condition head nouns were animate entities and resulted in high interpretability ratings. Some participants may have derived an understanding of these two items by imagining a fairytale like context with the animate ant and elephant, despite the general world-view that ants generally do not grill fish and that elephants generally do not cut paper.

Also, the head noun *megane* 'glasses' in *honya de hataraita megane* 'the glasses (which) worked at a bookstore' was commented as possibly being a nickname or a term referring to a person, and hence could be interpreted like a Core Condition item. In addition, the Other item *ronbun o kaita botoru* 'the bottle (which) wrote an article' was rated as interpretable for similar reasons. One comment about that particular survey item noted that it was possible to think of a context where the writer had difficulty coming up with the words to the article and used the power of a bottle of alcohol for inspiration. In that context, one could say that the bottle did write the bottle and would make such a construction easily interpretable, but it is due to the fact that the context also includes a writer.

One participant commented that "if one fantasizes or dreams of a situation, it is possible to think of every item as interpretable", and this sentiment can be seen in the individual item ratings generally not being 100% interpretable or uninterpretable.

5.3.2. Word choice

In the previous section, animacy was identified as a possible reason in influencing participants' interpretability ratings for Other Condition items. For instance, despite the head nouns *ari* 'ant' and *zoo* 'elephant' being semantically or pragmatically nonsensical in the construction, participants may have been influenced by the possibility of those nouns functioning as the subjects of the modifying clause. This kind of effect from word choice can be seen in several of the other items and suggests how participants reached their judgments.

For instance, in the Core Condition item *torusutoi o honyaku-sita bungakusya* 'the literary scholar (who) translated Tolstoy', while the predicate *honyaku-sita* 'translated' and head noun *bungakusya* 'literary scholar' seem to be reasonable associations, the activity of translation may be more commonly associated with translators than with scholars, resulting in some judgments of unacceptability. Item 2 in the Oblique Condition can be interpreted in a similar way. The construction, *tomato o tabeta nooen* 'the plantation (where) (someone) ate a tomato, may have suffered from lower ratings due to the unclear relation between 'eating tomatoes' and 'plantation'. The clause *tomato o tabeta* 'ate a tomato' evokes the true argument or core role of Eater or non-core, default arguments like Location. However, while *nooen* 'plantation' can occupy one of those roles, the possible interpretation of eating a tomato at a plantation was not borne out of the participant ratings. In fact, a Japanese consultant remarked on that unnaturalness, noting that *tomato* is not usually eaten at a *nooen* and suggesting that a more natural construction would be to replace *nooen* with *hatake* 'vegetable field' and to also change the predicate *tabeta* 'eat' with *saibai-sita* 'cultivated'. This can be contrasted with another Oblique Condition item, *ronbun o kaita heya* 'the room (where) (someone) wrote an article'. The predicate, *kaita* 'wrote', can be situated in a place and the head noun *heya* 'room' can occupy that slot more readily for that action unlike the *tabeta* and *nooen* case.

These cases serve as evidence that word choice and meaning influences the interpretability of Japanese NMCs. If we were to adopt an argument structure approach like Pustejovsky's (1995), having a head noun which fulfills an available argument of the predicate in the modifying clause should be easily understood as in the items presented in the Core Condition, regardless of whether the argument is obligatory or not. In one respect, the applicability of such an analysis is viable, as the data showed that items in the Core and Oblique Conditions were generally rated as highly interpretable. This is even more so if we consider that particular items, such as *gohan o tabeta otyawan* 'the rice bowl (someone used) to eat a meal' and *tomato o tabeta nooen* 'the plantation (where) (someone) ate a tomato' in the Oblique Condition, appeared to be less interpretable. As a result, an NMC's ease of construability depends on whether the relationship between the head noun and the modifying clause is meaningful and easily conceivable. While an argument structure approach can explain the meaningfulness relationship between the head noun and the predicate of the modifying clause, it seems less equipped to account for why some relationships are more readily construable than others. That is, it is useful to know what kinds of arguments are available, but it is even more useful to know the relationships of particular words that are able to occupy the available arguments or roles.

5.3.3. Summary

If the above reasoning is true, then an analysis of Japanese NMCs in an exclusively syntactic or semantic approach seems to have difficulty explaining the responses elicited in this study. However, a frame-semantic like approach in the vein of Fillmore's (e.g. 1982, 1992) frames as applied by Matsumoto (1997) seems to provide a comprehensive explanation to how Japanese NMCs are construed. Although Japanese NMCs do not explicitly mark the relation between the modifying clause and the head noun, the results of this study suggest that that relationship is derived by considering whether both the modifying clause and the head noun overlap in some meaningful way. This meaningfulness depends partly on word choice. That is, the construability of an NMC depends on identifying the relationships between the modifying clause and the head noun — whether the modifying clause hosts the head noun (similar to relative clauses, where the head noun fills a gapped relation in the predicate), the head noun hosts the modifying clause (as in *nioi* 'smell' in *sakana o yaku nioi* 'the smell of grilling fish'), or both the head noun and the modifying clause host the content of each other (as in *torustoi o honyaku-sita hoosyuu* 'the money (which) (resulted after) (someone) translated Tolstoy').

This study adds to the existing literature by examining the notion of a noun-modifying construction with an experimental approach. The results in this study provide empirical data to account for why some constructions are considered interpretable or not. By refining the methods given in this study, more data can be gathered to better understand the processes involved in NMC comprehension. Possible avenues of further studies include measuring participants' response times, eliciting word associations from predicates or head nouns, or determining how head nouns occupying different non-core roles affect the interpretability of NMCs. It is hoped that subsequent research will shed more light on the process of determining NMC interpretability.

From a typological perspective, the data, primarily from items in Core and Oblique Conditions, cast doubt on the applicability of the concept "relative clause" in Japanese. As the data suggest, Japanese NMCs can be analyzed as if they were "relative clauses" when the head nouns can be placed with a simple case marking into the modifying predicate. However, Japanese NMCs have functions beyond the relative clause construction, and so the concept falls short in explaining Japanese NMCs. The concept of relative clauses provides a point of departure to cross-linguistically compare Japanese NMCs with other constructions, but, as Haspelmath (2010) notes, a grammatical category like relative clauses "cannot be equated across languages" (p. 681). Indeed, one of the motivations of this study was to test how well the concept of a relative clause fits with the Japanese general noun-modifying construction, and the results of this study reinforce the notion that "relative clauses" do not hold up cross-linguistically, or at the very least for Japanese. In fact, there are many languages in Eurasia that employ a general noun-modifying clause construction, such as Korean, Mandarin, the Uralic language Tundra Nenets, and varieties of Nakh-Daghestanian languages (see Matsumoto, Comrie, & Sells, 2017). Relative clauses, however, can still be a useful notion and can be considered as but one strategy used by certain languages to perform noun modification. With regards to Japanese the notion of a relative clause accounts only for a limited number of functions of the general noun-modifying clause construction, so a broader grammatical category like NMC would be a more useful category.

In this study we have seen that the interpretability of Japanese NMCs depend on what appears to be a mixture of syntactic, semantic, and pragmatic information, and the data provide a strong indication that semantic and pragmatic cues play a major role in the interpretation of Japanese NMCs. This is especially the case since these constructions do not have an explicit cue marking the relationship between their head nouns and their modifying clauses.

6. Concluding remarks

One of starting points in the discussion of Japanese NMCs has been the viability of Keenan and Comrie's (1977) Accessibility Hierarchy in various languages and its claim that certain types of constructions are psychologically more easily comprehended than others. Since that time Japanese NMCs have been analyzed as a construction which behaves like relative clauses but functions in more ways beyond syntactic categories. This paper provides evidence that the interpretability of Japanese NMCs depend more on semantic and pragmatic information than syntactic information, especially since there are no overt syntactic markers to denote the relationship between the head noun and the modifying clause. In addition, syntactic categories like subject, direct object, or indirect object do not neatly predict the ease of interpretation. One possible way to better understand how this kind of information affects interpretability would be to conduct a follow-up study collecting response times from participants. What appears to be more important is the knowledge of available arguments evoked by words and the associations that can be derived from words.

From a typological perspective, this study casts doubt on the notion of relative clauses as an applicable cross-linguistic comparison, at least in the case of Japanese. If one adopts the concept of relative clauses when analyzing Japanese NMCs, it is possible to explain the behavior of a subset of these constructions. However, as the data show, Japanese NMCs that do not fit the characterization of a relative clause exhibit similar construability ratings, suggesting that a broader category like noun-modifying constructions may be a more productive description.

This paper provides one set of data which can be refined for future studies. For instance, although this paper set out to show if an NMC is interpretable or not, it does not specifically address NMCs having multiple interpretations. It would also be interesting to see how people from different languages or learning different languages understand constructions like NMCs. As presented in this paper, carefully controlling information about word associations, situational context, and world-view would shed more light on how people process language.

Acknowledgements

Thanks go to Yoshiko Matsumoto regarding experiment design and helpful feedback. My appreciation also goes out to the three anonymous reviewers for their comments that helped clarify and refine the paper. I also thank Michael Frank and Ben Peloquin for their assistance on data analysis as well as the Language and Cognition Lab for their support in conducting the experiment. Lastly, I thank Hanae Kaneko for assistance in data collection.

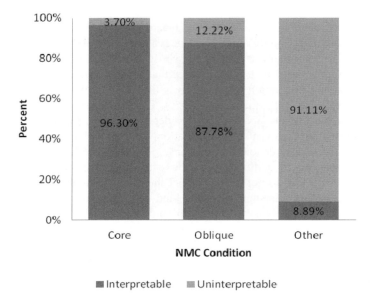

Figure 1. Rates of interpretability by each type of NMC

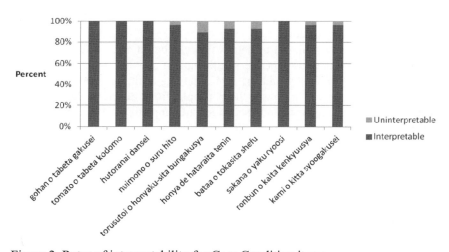

Figure 2. Rates of interpretability for Core Condition items

Interpretability of noun-modifying constructions in Japanese 23

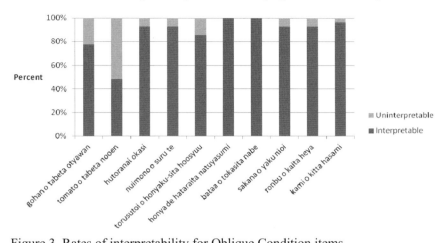

Figure 3. Rates of interpretability for Oblique Condition items

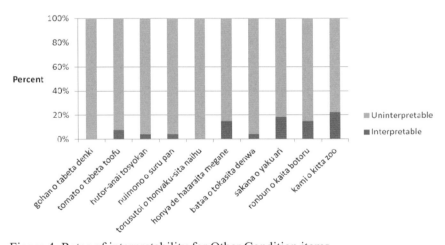

Figure 4. Rates of interpretability for Other Condition items

Appendix 1: Target noun-modifying constructions

Note about translations — each English translation is only one possible interpretation. Since the English translation forces a relative pronoun like who, which, or where or a relevant phrase, each translation contains parenthesis where these ambiguities may occur. The translations for the items in the Other Condition in particular sound strange due to a lack of semantic and pragmatic relation, but that is precisely one of the aims of that condition.

1) Core Condition: NMCs with semantically/pragmatically appropriate subject head nouns

    a) *[gohan   o   tabeta]   gakusei*
       meal   ACC   ate   student
       'the student (who) ate a meal'
    b) *[tomato   o   tabeta]   kodomo*
       tomato   ACC   ate   child
       'the child (who) ate a tomato'
    c) *[hutor-anai]   dansei*
       gain.weight-not   man
       'the man (who) does not become fat'
    d) *[nuimono o   suru]   hito*
       sewing   ACC   do   person
       'the person (who) sews'
    e) *[torusutoi o   honyaku-sita]   bungakusya*
       Tolstoy   ACC   translate-do:PAST   scholar
       'the literary scholar (who) translated Tolstoy'
    f) *[honya   de   hataraita]   tenin*
       bookstore at   worked   employee
       'the employee (who) worked at a bookstore'
    g) *[bataa   o   tokasita]   shefu*
       butter   ACC   melted   chef
       'the chef (who) melted butter'
    h) *[sakana o   yaku]   ryoosi*
       fish   ACC   grill   fisherman
       'the fisherman (who) grills fish'
    i) *[ronbun   o   kaita]   kenkyuusya*
       article   ACC   wrote   researcher
       'the researcher (who) wrote an article'
    j) *[kami   o   kitta]   syoogakusei*
       paper   ACC   cut   elementary.school.student
       'the elementary school student ( ) cut paper'

2) Oblique Condition: NMCs with semantically/pragmatically appropriate non-subject head nouns
    a) *[gohan   o   tabeta]   otyawan*
        meal   ACC   ate   rice.bowl
        'the rice bowl (with which (someone)) ate a meal'
    b) *[tomato   o   tabeta]   nooen*
        tomato   ACC   ate   plantation
        'the plantation (where) (someone) ate a tomato'
    c) *[hutor-anai]   okasi*
        gain.weight-not   sweets
        'the sweets (which when (someone) eats) does not become fat'
    d) *[nuimono   o   suru]   te*
        sewing   ACC   do   hand
        'the hand (of (someone) which) sews'
    e) *[torusutoi   o   honyaku-sita]   hoosyuu*
        Tolstoy   ACC   translate-do:PAST   payment
        'the money (which resulted after (someone)) translated Tolstoy'
    f) *[honya   de   hataraita]   natuyasumi*
        bookstore   at   worked   summer.vacation
        'the summer vacation (when (someone)) worked at a bookstore'
    g) *[bataa   o   tokasita]   nabe*
        butter   ACC   melted   sauce.pan
        'the saucepan (with which (someone)) melted butter'
    h) *[sakana   o   yaku]   nioi*
        fish   ACC   grill   smell
        'the smell (which results when (someone)) grills fish'
    i) *[ronbun   o   kaita]   heya*
        article   ACC   wrote   room
        'the room (where (someone)) wrote an article'
    j) *[kami   o   kitta]   hasami*
        paper   ACC   cut   scissors
        'the scissors (with which (someone)) cut paper'

3) Other Condition: NMCs with semantically/pragmatically unrelated predicates and head nouns
    a) *[gohan   o   tabeta]   denki*
        meal   ACC   ate   electric.light
        'the electric light (which) ate a meal'
    b) *[tomato   o   tabeta]   toofu*
        tomato   ACC   ate   tofu
        'the tofu (which) ate a tomato'

c) *[hutor-anai]*   *tosyokan*
    gain.weight-not   library
    'the library (which) does not become fat'

d) *[nuimono o suru] pan*
    sewing   ACC   do   bread
    'the bread (which) sews'

e) *[torusutoi o honyaku-sita] naihu*
    Tolstoy   ACC   translate-do:PAST   knife
    'the knife (which) translated Tolstoy'

f) *[honya de hataraita] megane*
    bookstore   at   worked   eyeglasses
    'the eyeglasses (which) worked at a bookstore'

g) *[bataa o tokasita] denwa*
    butter   ACC   melted   telephone
    'the telephone (which) melted butter'

h) *[sakana o yaku] ari*
    fish   ACC   grill   ant
    'the ant (which) grills fish'

i) *[ronbun o kaita] botoru*
    article   ACC   wrote   bottle
    'the bottle (which) wrote an article'

j) *[kami o kitta] zoo*
    paper   ACC   cut   elephant
    'the elephant (that) cut paper'

Appendix 2: Filler noun-modifying constructions

1) *[yatte-miyoo!] kenkyuujyo*
    do-try   laboratory
    'laboratory (that) will try'

2) *[syoobookan-ni nareru?!] gaido*
    firefighter-GOAL   become   guide
    'a guide (to) become a firefighter'

3) *[yooisite-itadakimasita] mono*
    prepare.do-receive:HON:POL:PAST   thing
    'things (we asked you to) prepare'

4) *[o-kai-ninari-masita] utuwa*
    HON-bought-HON-POL:PAST   bowl
    'bowl (that (someone)) bought'

5) *[yatta!]*   kan
    did   feeling
    'feeling (of having) done (something)!'
6) *[yamada-san ga   o-shiharai-ninari-masita]*   kingaku
    Yamada-Mr. NOM   HON-pay-HON-POL:PAST   sum.of.money
    'amount of money (that) Mr. Yamada paid'
7) *[ima   sore   ga   doko-ni   aru   yara]*
    now   that   NOM   where:LOC   exist   wonder
    jyootai
    situation
    'situation (where (someone)) wonders where that is now'
8) *[nani   yatte-nda]*   terebi
    what   doing-SE:NONPAST   television
    'television (where (someone)) is doing what'
9) *[mada   maniau]*   natu   no
    yet   be.in.time   summer   GEN
    kokunairyokoo
    domestic.travel
    'summer travel (where (someone)) is still on time'
10) *[o-mati-simasu]*   zikan
    HON-wait-do:POL   time
    'time (when (someone)) waits'
11) *[tikyuu   ga   marui]*   zizitu
    earth   NOM   round   fact
    'the fact (that) the earth is round'
12) *[koinu   ga   ame   no   mati   o   samayou]*
    puppy   NOM   rain   GEN   town   ACC   wander
    terebi   no   CM
    television   GEN   commercial
    'television commercial (where) a puppy wanders around a rainy town'
13) *[kamawanai tte]*   kanzi
    not.mind   COMP   feeling
    'feeling (that (someone)) does not mind
14) *[totemo   omosiro-katta]*   kioku
    very   interesting-was   memory
    'memory (where (something)) was very interesting'
15) *[atama   o   tataku]*   kuse
    head   ACC   hit   habit
    'habit (of) hitting (one's) head'
16) *[karada   o   wakagaeraseru   toiu]*   kenkyuu
    body   ACC   make.young.again   COMP   research
    'research (which) rejuvenates one's body'

17) *[kokoro   o   yurusiteiru   toiu]   insyoo*
    heart   ACC   confiding   COMP   impression
    'impression (of) confiding (someone's) heart'
18) *[buka   ga   jyoosi   o   erabu   toiu]   hassoo*
    subordinate   NOM   superior ACC   choose   COMP   idea
    'idea (that) subordinates choose their superiors'
19) *[inu   ni   osow-areru   toiu]   ziken*
    dog   by   chase-be   COMP   case
    'case (where (someone)) is chased by a dog'
20) *[kikai   o   ataer-arena-katta   toiu]   riyuu*
    chance   ACC   give-PASS-not   COMP   reason
    'reason (for) not being given a chance'
21) *[kinen-site-yokatta]   koto*
    quit.smoking-do-was.good   thing
    'the fact (that) quitting smoking was good'
22) *[oisikatta]   mono*
    was.delicious   thing
    'thing (which) was delicious'
23) *[tenisu   o   suru]   no*
    tennis   ACC   do   thing
    'the fact (that (someone)) plays tennis'
24) *[doroboo   ga   nige-teiku]   tokoro*
    thief   NOM   escape-to   place
    'place (where) the thief escapes to'
25) *[zeeritu   ga   yasukatta]   wake*
    tariff   NOM   was.inexpensive   reason
    'reason (for) the tariff being inexpensive'
26) *[maeni   hayatteita]   yatsu*
    before   was.popular   thing
    'thing that was popular before'
27) *[rirakkusu-si-tai]   toki*
    relax-do-want   time
    'time (when (someone)) wants to relax'
28) *[tiisai]   koro*
    small   period
    'period (when (someone) was) young'
29) *[zibun   yori   mawari   no   hito   no]   hoo*
    oneself   than   surrounding   GEN   person   GEN   side
    'the side (of) people rather than one's self'
30) *[kodukaikasegi   o   suru]   tame*
    earning.allowance   ACC   do   purpose
    'purpose (of) earning allowance'

References

Bates, D., Maechler, M., Bolker, B., & Walker, S. (2015). Fitting linear mixed-effects models using lme4. *Journal of Statistical Software, 67*(1), 1-48. doi:10.18637/jss.v067.i01.

Brown, D. (1971). Children's comprehension of relativized English sentences. *Child Development, 42*, 1923-1936.

Comrie, B. (1996). The unity of noun modifying clauses in Asian languages. *Pan-Asiatic Linguistics: Proceedings of the Fourth International Symposium on Languages and Linguistics*, January 8-10, Vol. 3, 1077-1088.

Comrie, B. (1998). Rethinking the typology of relative clauses. *Language Design, 1*, 59-86.

Comrie, B. (2002). Typology and language acquisition: The case of relative clauses. In A. Ramat (Ed.), *Typology and second language acquisition* (pp. 19-37).

de Villiers, J., Tager-Flusberg, H., Hakuta, K., & Cohen, M. (1979). Children's comprehension of relative clauses. *Journal of Psycholinguistic Research, 8*, 499–518.

Diessel, H. & Tomasello, M. (2000). The development of relative clauses in spontaneous child speech. *Cognitive Linguistics, 11*, 131-151.

Diessel, H. & Tomasello, M. (2005). A new look at the acquisition of relative clauses. *Language, 81*, 1-25.

Fillmore, C. (1982). Frame semantics. In The Linguistic Society of Korea (Ed.), *Linguistics in the morning calm* (pp. 111–138). Seoul: Hanshin.

Fillmore, C. J. & Atkins, B. T. (1992). Toward a frame-based lexicon: The semantics of RISK and its neighbors. In A. Lehrer & E. F. Kittay (Eds.), *Frames, fields, and contrasts* (pp. 75-102). Hillsdale, NJ: Lawrence Erlbaum.

Haspelmath, M. (2010). Comparative concepts and descriptive categories in crosslinguistic studies. *Language, 86*(3), 663–687.

Iwasaki, S. (2013). *Japanese: Revised edition*. Amsterdam/Philadelphia: John Benjamins.

Keenan, E. & Comrie, B. (1977). Noun phrase accessibility and universal grammar. *Linguistic Inquiry, 8*(1), 63-99.

Kidd, E. & Bavin, E. (2002). English-speaking children's comprehension of relative clauses: Evidence for general-cognitive and language-specific constraints on development. *Journal of Psycholinguistic Research, 31*, 599–617.

Martin, S. E. (1975). *A reference grammar of Japanese*. Honolulu: University of Hawaii Press.

Matsumoto, Y. (1988). Semantics and pragmatics of noun-modifying constructions in Japanese. *Proceedings of the Fourteenth Annual Meeting of the Berkeley Linguistics Society*, 166-175.

Matsumoto, Y. (1997). *Noun-modifying constructions in Japanese: A frame-semantic approach.* Amsterdam/Philadelphia: John Benjamins.

Matsumoto, Y. (2007). Integrating frames: Complex noun phrase constructions in Japanese. In S. Kuno, S. Makino, & S. Strauss (Eds.), *Aspects of Linguistics: In Honor of Noriko Akatsuka (Gengogaku no Syosoo: Akatsuka Noriko Kyoozyu Kinen Ronbunsyuu)*, (pp. 131–154). Tokyo: Kurosio.

Matsumoto, Y. (2010). Interactional frames and grammatical descriptions: The case of Japanese noun-modifying constructions. *Constructions and Frames, 2*(2), 135–157.

Matsumoto, Y. (2017). General noun-modifying clause constructions in Japanese. In Y. Matsumoto, B. Comrie, & P. Sells (Eds.), *Noun-modifying clause constructions in languages of Eurasia: Rethinking theoretical and geographical boundaries* (pp. 23–44). Amsterdam/Philadelphia: John Benjamins.

Matsumoto, Y., Comrie, B., & Sells, P. (Eds.) (2017). *Noun-modifying clause constructions in languages of Eurasia: Rethinking theoretical and geographical boundaries.* Amsterdam/Philadelphia: John Benjamins.

Ozeki, H. & Shirai, Y. (2007). The consequences of variation in the acquisition of relative clauses: An analysis of longitudinal production data from five Japanese children. In Y. Matsumoto, D. Y. Oshima, O. W. Robinson, & P. Sells (Eds.) *Diversity and language: Perspectives and implications* (pp. 243–270). Stanford, CA: CSLI.

Pustejovsky, J. (1995). *The generative lexicon.* Cambridge, MA/London: The MIT Press.

Qualtrics [computer software]. (2015). Provo, UT. Available from http://www.qualtrics.com.

Tavakolian, S. L. (1981). The conjoined-clause analysis of relative clauses. In S. L. Tavakolian (Ed.), *Language acquisition and linguistic theory* (pp. 167–187). Cambridge: The MIT Press.

R Core Team (2014). R: A language and environment for statistical computing. R Foundation for Statistical Computing, Vienna, Austria. URL http://www.R-project.org/.

Sheldon, A. (1974). The role of parallel function in the acquisition of relative clauses in English. *Journal of Verbal Learning and Verbal Behavior, 13*, 272–281.

Wang, L., Horie, K., & Pardeshi, P. (2009). Toward a functional typology of noun modifying constructions in Japanese and Chinese: A corpus-based account. *Studies in Language Sciences, 8*, 213–228. Tokyo: Kurosio.

Yip, V. & Matthews, S. (2007). Relative clauses in Cantonese-English bilingual children. *Studies in Second Language Acquisition, 29*, 277–300. doi: 10.1017/S0272263107070143.

日本語における名詞修飾構造の解釈可能性

ポール・ガニア（スタンフォード大学）

要旨

日本語における名詞修飾構造とは、一般的な構造であるにも関わらず関係節、または名詞同格節のように多種多様な意味を表し得るものである。従来の統語論・意味論・語用論に基盤を置く研究は、一つの構造からどのようにこれらの意味が派生されるかを分析してきた（例えば、Keenan & Comrie, 1977; Comrie, 1996, 1998; Matsumoto, 1988, 1997, 2007）。本稿では、実験による調査データを通して、どのように統語論的・意味論的・語用論的な情報が名詞修飾構文の解釈の成立に寄与するかを解明したものである。30項目の解釈可否の評価種目を設けることにより、アンケート調査の参加者は、名詞修飾構文を解釈するために統語的・意味的・語用的情報を集約することが分かった。この分析の結果、日本語では、名詞修飾構文の解釈が成立するか否かは、単語の選択と、修飾節と主名詞の間に妥当な関係の解釈が導きだせるかにより依存していることが示唆された。また、本研究は言語類型論の観点から、「関係節」の概念が通言語的比較のために適用可能か否かという疑問を投げかける。

Children's syntactic positional knowledge of a quantifier in Japanese

Emi CALEY-KOMINE, Meiji Gakuin University

Abstract
First language acquisition looks effortless: we all know from experience that children learn new words at an astonishing rate although it is a struggle for adults to learn new words in a second language. How do children learn new words? This paper presents evidence of syntactic bootstrapping from Japanese data. Children use syntax to guide word learning. There is a syntactic positional difference between an adjective and a quantifier when they modify nominals in Japanese. A quantifier can appear either in a prenominal position or in a postnominal position, while an adjective can appear in a prenominal position but not in a postnominal position. Through an experiment with a picture verification task, this study reveals that Japanese- speaking children at around age four have syntactic knowledge of the positional difference between an adjective and a quantifier. Furthermore, the positional information helps them to determine the meaning of a new word.

1. Introduction

It seems that children learn new words with ease while it is difficult for adults to learn new words in a second language. They expand their vocabulary at a remarkable rate. The average child has learned over fourteen thousand words by age six, which means that children learn about nine new words a day from the age of eighteen months, since vocabulary growth does not begin in earnest until about that age (Carey, 1978). How do they learn new words at such an astonishing rate? Some researchers propose that children are guided by internal biases and assumptions (see Pinker, 1989; Fisher, Gertner, Scott, & Yuan, 2010). One example is syntactic bootstrapping, and evidence of it is presented in this paper. That is, syntax guides Japanese-speaking children when they assign a quantifier interpretation to a new word.

2. Syntactic bootstrapping

Research has shown that children use syntax to guide word learning through a process, which is called syntactic bootstrapping (see Fisher, Gertner, Scott & Yuan, 2010). Syntactic bootstrapping predicts that, once a child has mastered the word order and used it to interpret sentences in his or her language, syntax constrains and directs the child's interpretation of new words.

Gertner, Fisher, and Eisengart (2006) showed that English-speaking two-year-olds use word order to interpret sentences containing unknown verbs. In their experiment, they showed children two videos simultaneously side-by-side on the screens. In the videos, a girl and a boy engaged in caused motion events. The girl performed as an agent in one video, and as a patient in the other. While watching the videos, children heard a stimulus sentence as in (1).

(1) The girl is *gorping* the boy.

In the test, children looked longer at the video in which the girl was an agent of the novel action. This result indicated that the children had abstract representations of linguistic knowledge. Whatever the new word meant, they correctly inferred by using knowledge of English word order that the subject in the sentence was an agent and the object in the sentence was a patient.

Fisher, Klingler, and Song (2006) reported that two-year-olds use sentence structures to learn new prepositions. In their experiment, they also showed side-by-side videos. In the first phase, children watched a hand pointing at a toy duck on a box in both videos. Half the number of participants (the noun condition group) heard a stimulus sentence containing a novel word that was presented as a noun as in (2a). The other half (the preposition condition group) heard a stimulus sentence containing a novel word that was presented as a preposition as in (2b).

(2) a. This is *a corp*.
     b. This is *acorp* my box.

In the testing phase, two different events were presented on the screens. One screen showed a new duck next to the box (object-match), and the other screen showed toy glasses on the box (location-match). A hand pointed to another duck on the box on both screens. Children in the noun condition group heard a test sentence as in (3a) and those in the preposition condition group heard a test sentence as in (3b).

(3) a. This is *a corp*. What else is *a corp*?
     b. This is *acorp* my box. What else is *acorp* my box?

In the test, children in each group looked at the matching picture longer. That is, children in the noun condition group looked at the object-matching screen longer, while children in the preposition condition group looked at the location-matching screen longer. The result shows that adding a noun after an unknown word informed the children that it described a spatial relation.

In the current article, I present further evidence of syntactic bootstrapping, showing that Japanese syntax can constrain the interpretation of a new quantifier. I demonstrate that syntactic positional information can be a cue for Japanese-speaking children to determine the meaning of a new word. An experiment with a picture verification task reveals that, at around age four, Japanese-speaking children have syntactic knowledge of the positional difference between an adjective and a quantifier. Furthermore, the positional information helps them in deciding the meaning of a new word.

3. Syntactic constraint on an adjective in Japanese

There is a syntactic positional difference between an adjective and a quantifier in Japanese. Japanese grammar allows a quantifier to appear in either a prenominal position or a postnominal position as in sentences (4). When a quantifier is in a postnominal position, it is sometimes called a Quantifier Float (QF).

(4) a. *Koppu-ni   takusan   mizu-ga   hai-tte(i)ru   yo.*
       glass-in   a lot   water-$_{NOM}$ filled-be
       "There is a lot of water in the glass."
    b. *Koppu-ni   mizu-ga   takusan   hai-tte(i)ru   yo.*
       glass-in   water-$_{NOM}$ a lot   filled-be
       "There is a lot of water in the glass."

In sentence (4a), *takusan* is a quantifier meaning 'a lot' and *mizu-ga* is a nominative-marked noun meaning 'water'. The meaning of the whole sentence is "there is a lot of water in the glass." In sentence (4b), the quantifier *takusan* is in a postnominal position. This sentence is grammatically correct and has the same meaning as sentence (4a).

Meanwhile, Japanese grammar allows a noun modifying adjective to appear only in a prenominal position (see Huang & Ochi, 2014), as in sentences (5).

(5) a. *Koppu-ni   aoi   mizu-ga   hai-tte(i)ru   yo.*
       glass-in   blue   water-$_{NOM}$ filled-be
       "There is blue water in the glass."
    b. **Koppu-ni   mizu-ga   aoi   hai-tte(i)ru   yo.*
       glass-in   water-$_{NOM}$ blue   filled-be
       "There is blue water in the glass."

In sentence (5a), *aoi* is an adjective meaning 'blue'. The meaning of the whole sentence is "there is blue water in the glass." The only difference between sentences (5a) and (5b) is the position of the adjective *aoi*. In sentence (5b), the adjective *aoi* is in the postnominal position. This sentence is grammatically incorrect.

In short, a quantifier can appear in a postnominal position in Japanese, but an adjective cannot.

(6) Japanese syntactic constraint on an adjective:
An adjective cannot appear in a postnominal position as a noun modifier.[1]

Some questions follow from this syntactic constraint. Do Japanese-speaking children know the syntactic positional difference between a quantifier and an adjective? Are they able to exploit this knowledge to learn a new word?

4. Experiment
4.1. Materials

The novel word *nekeroi* was used in the experiment. It is not a real Japanese word, but it ends with the *-i* form[2]. The *-i* form makes it sound natural as a modifier in Japanese because the *-i* form is very common for Japanese adjectives. Moreover, there are some quantifiers that end with the *-i* form as well, but not many[3].

When the novel word *nekeroi* is interpreted as an adjective, it refers to a property such as color, size, or texture. I call this Adjective Interpretation. Meanwhile, when it is interpreted as a quantifier, with a meaning such as 'a lot,' 'many,' 'a few,' or 'a little,' I call this Quantifier Interpretation.

In sentence (7a), *nekeroi* is in a prenominal position. Since either an adjective or a quantifier can appear in a prenominal position, Japanese grammar allows both the Adjective Interpretation and the Quantifier Interpretation for this sentence. In other words, *nekeroi* could refer to either a property or a quantity in sentence (7a). On the other hand, when *nekeroi* is in a postnominal position as in sentence (7b), the Adjective Interpretation is not allowed. Therefore, *nekeroi* can refer to only a quantity in this sentence.

(7) a. *Koppu-ni   nekeroi   mizu-ga   hai-te(i)ru   yo.*
      glass-in   *nekeroi*   water-$_{NOM}$ filled-be
      "There is *nekeroi* water in the glass."   AI/QI

---

[1] A reviewer pointed out that an adjective appears postnominally in a secondary predicate although in that case it is not a modifier. The verb used in the experiment does not take a secondary predicate. Therefore, an adjective cannot appear in a postnominal position. When a different verb is tested, the rate of Adjective Interpretation might increase.

[2] Some Japanese speakers pointed out that the *-i* form might cause a bias because it sounds more like an adjective than a quantifier. However, this actually makes the results more interesting. Even though it may be phonetically biased, Japanese-speaking children interpret the novel word as a quantifier by using syntactic knowledge (see the results).

[3] For instance, *ippai* is a quantifier that ends with the *-i* form and means 'a lot.'

b. *Koppu-ni   mizu-ga   nekeroi   hai-tte(i)ru   yo.*[4]
   glass-in   water-$_{NOM}$ nekeroi   filled-be
   "There is *nekeroi* water in the glass."   *AI/QI

Generally, when a child encounters a new word, the possible interpretations are countless. In the experiment, *nekeroi* has two possible interpretations: the Adjective Interpretation and the Quantifier Interpretation.[5] If children know the syntactic constraint (6) and it guides them in the course of word learning, we can predict that Japanese-speaking children will not assign the Adjective Interpretation to the novel word when it appears in a postnominal position, even if it is the first time they hear the word.

4.2. Procedure

A picture verification task was employed in order to find out if children know the difference between an adjective and a quantifier and if they can assign a meaning to a novel word by using positional information. The experiment consists of two phases, a training phase and a testing phase. In the training phase, the novel word *nekeroi* is introduced. An experimenter shows some pictures to a puppet and a child. Two glasses are depicted in each picture. The glass on the right has a blue mark. One of the glasses always contains a lot of pinkish water and the other glass contains a little purplish water. At first, the experimenter explains that the glass with the blue mark is the puppet's glass. Then the puppet, which is manipulated by another experimenter, makes a comment for each picture as in sentences (8). After making a comment, the puppet tells the child that he likes the picture when the glass with the blue mark contains a lot of pinkish water, and that he does not like the picture when the glass with the blue mark contains a small quantity of purplish water (Figure 1). The experimenter shows six pictures to a child in this phase. Three of the pictures are commented by the puppet as in (8a), and the other three pictures are commented as in (8b).

---

[4] A reviewer pointed out that the same outcome would be obtained even if a child ignored the novel word. In order to ensure that the child perceives the novel word, another test sentence that does not contain the novel word needs to be tested.

[5] There are thousands of possible interpretations for a new word. I assume that children determine the meaning of a new word not only by using linguistic information but also by using non-linguistic information. In the experiment, the presented picture leaves two possibilities of interpretation, AI and QI, and the syntactic positional information helps the children to decide which interpretation they assign.

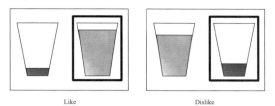

Figure 1. Pictures used in the training phase.

(8) a. *Boku-no koppu-ni mizu-ga   nekeroi hai-tteru yo.*
      my   glass-in   water-$_{NOM}$ nekeroi filled-be
      "There is *nekeroi* water in my glass."
    b. *Boku-no koppu-ni mizu-ga   nekeroi hai-tte   nai yo.*
      my   glass-in   water-$_{NOM}$ nekeroi filled-be NEG
      "There is not *nekeroi* water in my glass."

In the experiment, there are two possible interpretations for the novel word *nekeroi*: the Adjective Interpretation, meaning 'pinkish,' and the Quantifier Interpretation, meaning 'a lot.' Both the interpretations do not contradict the situation. That is, the word *nekeroi* is ambiguous in this situation. However, in the test sentences, *nekeroi* appears in a postnominal position. If children have the syntactic knowledge that an adjective does not appear in a postnominal position in Japanese, they should be guided to abandon the Adjective Interpretation.

After the training phase introduces the novel word *nekeroi*, the testing phase examines how the children interpret it. The experimenter tells a child that she wants to collect only those pictures that the puppet likes and that she needs the child's help to choose the pictures. The experimenter reveals the test pictures one by one and asks the child if the puppet likes each picture or not. The pictures that the child chooses as the puppet's favorites are to be given to the puppet later. Crucial pictures show a lot of purplish water in a glass with a blue mark (Figure 2). If children are following the Adjective Interpretation, it is predicted that they will not choose the crucial pictures as the puppet's favorites since the glass with the blue mark does not contain pinkish water. On the other hand, if they are following the Quantifier Interpretation, it is predicted that they will choose the crucial pictures as the puppet's favorites since the glass with the blue mark contains a lot of water.

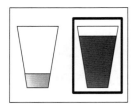

Figure 2. A crucial picture used in the testing phase.

Table 1 illustrates the predictions about children's responses. If they are using the Adjective Interpretation, they will choose pictures like (2) and not like (1). If they are using the Quantifier Interpretation, they will choose pictures like (1) and not like (2). Some filler pictures are included as shown in (3) and (4).

Table 1. Prediction

	(1)	(2)	(3)/(4)
Adjective Interpretation	✗	✓	✓ / ✗ (filler)
Quantifier Interpretation	✓	✗	✓ / ✗ (filler)

Ten pictures are presented in total in the testing phase. Three of them are type (1) in Table 1, another three are type (2) and the remaining four are filler pictures as in (3) and (4).

In addition to this target test, a control test was conducted. The control test uses the same materials and procedure as the target test; it differs only in its test sentences. In the training phase, children in the control group hear test sentences as in (9).

(9) a. *Boku-no   koppu-ni   nekeroi   mizu-ga   hai-tteru   yo.*
       my   glass-in   nekeroi   water-_{NOM} filled-be
       "There is *nekeroi* water in my glass."
   b. *Boku-no   koppu-ni   nekeroi   mizu-ga   hai-tte   nai   yo.*
       my   glass-in   nekeroi   water-_{NOM} filled-be NEG
       "There is not *nekeroi* water in my glass."

Here, the novel word *nekeroi* is in the prenominal position. Therefore, Japanese grammar allows both the Adjective Interpretation and the Quantifier Interpretation of the sentences.

If children can determine the meaning of the novel word by using the syntactic knowledge (6), it is predicted that children in the target group will show the Quantifier Interpretation of the novel word, while those in the control group will show the Adjective Interpretation more often than those in the target group do.

4.3. Participants

Twenty-one Japanese-speaking monolingual children were examined. They were recruited from day-care centers in Kanagawa and Tokyo. Of them, thirteen children participated in the target test and the other eight participated in the control test. Their age range was from 3;6 to 5;4. The mean age was 4;5. They were examined individually in a quiet room. It took less than ten minutes for each child to accomplish the whole trial.

Eight native Japanese-speaking adults were also tested as the control group. Their age range was from 21 to 24 years. They were recruited at Meiji Gakuin University. Four of them participated in the target test and the other four participated in the control test.

4.4. Results

The results showed that the children in the target group followed the Quantifier Interpretation at the rate of 78.2% (61/78). A t-test revealed that there was a significant difference between the Quantifier Interpretation and the Adjective Interpretation in the target group ($p<.001$, $t=6.922$). The children in the control group followed the Adjective Interpretation at the rate of 64.6% (31/48). A t-test revealed that there was a significant difference between the two interpretations in the control group as well ($p<.001$, $t=5.369$). Please note that, in the control test, Japanese grammar allows both the Adjective Interpretation and the Quantifier Interpretation. That is, although both interpretations are possible, Japanese-speaking children tended to interpret the novel word *nekeroi* as an adjective when it was in a prenominal position.[6] However, when it was in a postnominal position, they interpreted it as a quantifier. This indicates that syntactic positional information guided them in determining the meaning of the novel word.[7]

---

[6] It is assumed that the novel word's -*i* form might cause Japanese-speaking children to interpret it as an adjective (see footnote 1 on this point also). However, the fact that this phonetic bias is overcome by the syntactic position makes the results of this study more robust.

[7] A reviewer pointed out that the children in the experiment use not only knowledge of

These results from the children were similar to those of the adult natives. The adult participants in the target group followed the Quantifier Interpretation 75% of the time (18/24), while those in the control group followed the Adjective Interpretation 75% of the time (18/24). Like the children, they tended to interpret the novel word as a quantifier when it was in a postnominal position, but as an adjective when it was in a prenominal position (though both interpretations are possible in the latter case).

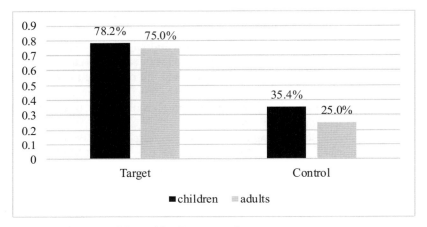

Figure 3. The rate of Quantifier Interpretation

5. Conclusion

There is a positional difference as to where an adjective and a quantifier can appear as a noun modifier in Japanese. Japanese syntax allows a quantifier to be in a postnominal position; however, it forbids an adjective from appearing in a postnominal position. The experiment that I conducted showed that Japanese-speaking children of about age four have syntactic knowledge of the positional difference between an adjective and a quantifier. Moreover, the experiment demonstrated that they are able to access this syntactic knowledge

---

syntactic position but also information that the test sentence does not contain genitive *-no*. In Japanese, when an element followed by genitive *-no* precedes a noun, grammar allows either AI or QI. When a test sentence contains genitive *-no*, the rate of QI might increase.
Eg. i) *Aoiro-no   mizu*
    blue color-$_{GEN}$ water
    "Blue water"
  ii) *Takusan-no   mizu*
    a lot-$_{GEN}$ water
    "A lot of water"

when determining the meaning of a novel word.

In the experiment, a novel word *nekeroi* was introduced to a child by an experimenter in the training phase. The word *nekeroi* has a morphologically appropriate form for both an adjective and a quantifier. The testing phase examined how the child interpreted the novel word. When *nekeroi* was in a postnominal position, the Adjective Interpretation was avoided and the participants followed the Quantifier Interpretation most of the time. Meanwhile, when *nekeroi* was in a prenominal position, the Adjective Interpretation was preferred even though both interpretations were possible. The results showed that syntax guided the children in determining the meaning of *nekeroi*.

Some questions, however, still remain. First, how do children learn the syntactic positional difference between an adjective and a quantifier? The example in (10) shows an NP structure. Since Japanese is a head-final language, a noun (the modified) always follows an adjective (the modifier).

(10)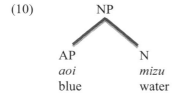
      AP   N
      aoi   *mizu*
      blue   water

Meanwhile, a numeral quantifier can appear in various locations in Japanese. There has been much discussion about how a sentence with a floating quantifier, such as (11b), derives.

(11) a. *Kinoo*   [*san-nin-no*   *kasyu*]*-ga*   *utat-ta.*
       yesterday [three-$_{CL}$-$_{GEN}$ singer]-$_{NOM}$ sing-$_{PAST}$
       "Three singers sang yesterday."
    b. *Kasyu-ga*   *kinoo*   *san-nin*   *utat-ta.*
       singer-$_{NOM}$ yesterday three-$_{CL}$ sing-$_{PAST}$

(Nakanishi, 2008)

There are two views about this issue: the stranding view and the adverb view. According to the stranding view, an NP moves somewhere higher in the structure and leaves a numeral behind. According to the adverb view, a numeral is base generated as an adjunct to a verbal projection, just like an adverb. If we adopt the stranding view of numeral quantifiers to quantity quantifiers, what children have to learn is the lexical optional information that a numeral quantifier and a quantity quantifier can be floated. If we take the adverb view, what children have to learn is the syntactic structure of adverbs.

Finally, though I have presented further evidence of syntactic bootstrapping, it is still unclear to what extent syntactic bootstrapping contributes to word learning. We saw that syntax guides children in determining the interpretation of a new word. However, this does not mean that children always or only depend on syntactic cues in learning new words. Moreover, the child participants in the experiment are at around age four. They might be over the period of vocabulary explosion. In order to investigate if they actually exploit the knowledge to acquire a new quantifier, younger children need to be tested. I leave these issues for further research.

Acknowledgments

I am grateful to Tetsuya Sano, Takuya Goro, Ken Hiraiwa, and members of Tokyo Psycholinguistic Laboratory, as well as to the audience at the 18th Annual International Conference of the Japanese Society for Language Sciences, held at the University of Tokyo on June 4 to 5, 2016, for their helpful comments and insights. I thank the teachers at the day-care centers who showed their understanding of the research and allowed me to conduct the experiment. I also thank Yoshiki Fujiwara, Ami Kawai, and Rumi Komine for their assistance in conducting the experiment. I would like to express my gratitude to the associate editor Mineharu Nakayama and the SLS reviewers as well for their comments that improved the manuscript.

References

Carey, S. (1978). The child as word learner. In M. Halle, J. Bresnan, & G. Miller (Eds.), *Linguistic theory and psychological reality* (pp. 264–293). Cambridge, MA: MIT Press.

Fisher, C., Gertner, Y., Scott, R. M., & Yuan, S. (2010). Syntactic bootstrapping. *WIREs Cognitive Science, 1*(2), 143–149.

Fisher, C., Klingler, S., & Song, H. (2006). What does syntax say about space? 26-month-olds use sentence structure in learning spatial terms. *Cognition, 101*(1), B19–B29.

Gertner, Y., Fisher, C., & Eisengart, J. (2006). Learning words and rules: Abstract knowledge of word order in early sentence comprehension. *Psychological Science, 17*(8), 684–691.

Huang, C.-T. J. & Ochi, M. (2014). Remarks on classifiers and nominal structure in East Asian. In C.-T. J. Huang & F.-H. Liu (Eds.), *Peaches and Plums* (pp. 53–74). Taipei: Academia Sinica.

Nakanishi, K. (2008). The syntax and semantics of floating quantifiers. In S. Miyagawa & M. Saito (Eds.), *The Oxford handbook of Japanese linguistics* (pp. 287–319). Oxford: Oxford University Press.

Pinker, S. (1989). *Learnability and cognition.* Cambridge, MA: MIT Press.

子どもの日本語における数量詞の統語位置の知識

ケイリー　絵美（明治学院大学）

要旨

なぜ幼い子どもは短期間で多くの単語を学習することが可能なのだろうか。本研究では日本語の実験結果から子どもが統語知識を利用して新規語の意味を推測することが可能であるということを示す。日本語では、名詞修飾語の数量詞は名詞の前あるいは後ろに現れることができるが、形容詞は名詞の前にしか現れることができない。実験を通し、日本語を母語とする4歳前後の子どもが数量詞と形容詞の統語的位置の違いを理解し、さらに初めて聞く単語（数量詞）の意味を決定する際に、この位置情報を利用することができることを示す。

北京在住日中国際結婚家庭の言語使用に関する一考察：家庭言語政策の枠組みを用いて

柳瀬千惠美（九州大学・日本学術振興会特別研究員 DC）

要旨

　北京在住日中国際結婚家庭の言語使用についてのインタビュー調査では、緩やかな双方向の「一親一言語」状況が多く確認された。そして家族言語政策の枠組みによる分析の結果、少数言語話者の親の言語に関する信念と家庭内役割が子どもの少数言語使用を促していること、とりわけ少数言語親と子の密接な関係が子どもの少数言語使用に寄与していることが示唆された。

1. はじめに

　グローバル化の進展により、多言語・多文化能力を持つ人材の育成が喫緊の課題となっているが、その一方でグローバル化がもたらしたものとして国際結婚の急増がある。二言語・二文化能力の発達を促す上で、国際結婚家庭はそれぞれの親の母語である二言語を自然習得する環境が備わっているという点で非常に有利であると考えられる。勿論、言語は家庭だけで習得するものではなく、個人の内面や外部の影響を抜きにしては語れないが、国際結婚家庭の事例研究の増加がバイリンガリズム研究に多くの示唆を与えることが期待される。

　日本人の国際結婚は、1980年代から急増し2000年代半ばピークに達し国内婚姻登録数の6%を占めた[1]が、リーマンショック後急減した後安定傾向を見せている。急増した国際結婚の中で大きな割合を占めるのが日中の組み合わせであり[2]、中国の経済発展に伴い日本在住家庭の中国移住も少なくない。しかしながら中国在住日中国際結婚家庭での言語使用についての事例研究はほとんどなく、その点で本研究の意義は大きいものと考える。

2. 先行研究

　国際結婚の増加を背景に、家庭で子どもをバイリンガルに育てるためには「一親一言語」（One parent-one language, 以下OPOL）原則[3]が有効であるという言説が広まりつつある（岡崎, 2011; Palviainen & Boyd, 2013; Piller, 2001）。

---

[1] 厚生労働省人口動態調査 http://www.estat.go.jp/SG1/estat/NewList.do?tid=000001028897

[2] 2015年現在、国内外登録を合算した国際結婚婚姻総数のうち、日本人男性と中国人女性の婚姻と中国人男性と日本人女性の婚姻はそれぞれ20.7%、4.7%を占める。厚生労働省人口動態調査及び人口動態統計確定数保管統計表（報告書非掲載表）上記のサイト及び http://www.e-stat.go.jp/SG1/estat/OtherList.do?bid=000001041663&cycode=7

[3] "One person-one language" とも言い、バイリンガル育成のための原則、政策、戦略、方略、アプローチの一つとされる。

OPOLとは、親が一人一言語で子どもに接することで、子どもの言語の使い分けが明確となり、二言語の習得を促進するという親から子どもへの言語使用の態度である。OPOLは、複数言語環境下での家庭におけるバイリンガリズム研究のテーマとして研究され、子どものバイリンガル発達に対する有効性を巡って論争が展開されてきた（Genesee, 2006; King & Fogle, 2013）。

　OPOLを強力に擁護するDöpke (1998) は、少数言語に対する社会的なサポートが少ない、またはサポートがない条件の下ではOPOLは重要であると主張するが、それに批判や疑念を抱く研究者もいる。Döpke (1998) によると、OPOLに対する批判や疑念は以下の3つに分類できる。一つはOPOLをエリートの非典型的な条件の下で行われるバイリンガリズムであるとする社会派からの批判である。二つめはOPOLが子どものバイリンガル発達を自動的に保証するわけではないという言語習得の立場からの批判である（Yamamoto, 2001a, 2001b; De Houwer, 2007）。また多くは、言語混合やコードスイッチングがバイリンガルのコミュニケーションの自然なあり方であり、それに対しOPOLは自然な会話に人工的で不必要な制限を設けるものであると批判する。

　Yamamoto (2001a, 2001b) は、日本在住の日本語―英語家族118家族のデータをもとにして、OPOL使用が有効かどうかを分析した結果、OPOL使用が必ずしも子どもの活発な少数言語使用を保証するものではなく、むしろ、子どもと少数言語との関わりが多ければ多いほど、子どもはこれを使用する可能性が高いと考察している。De Houwer (2007) は、ベルギーのオランダ語圏のフランドルでバイリンガル家庭を大規模に調査した結果、少なくとも一方の親が非オランダ語を話している1,899家庭において、その4分の1近くの家庭では子どもはオランダ語しか話さないことを報告し、OPOL戦略はインプットの必要条件でもなければ十分条件でもないと結論づけている。しかしながら、これらの量的調査では家庭での実際の使用状況の詳細やそれをもたらす要因について明確にすることは難しいと思われる。

　これに関連して、Yamamoto（2002, 2005, 2008）は国際結婚家庭の二言語の組み合わせに注目し、日本在住の日本語―英語と日本語―非英語の家庭の言語使用を調査した。その結果、二言語の組み合わせによって言語使用形態が大きく異なり、それは主として親の言語に関する考え方とホスト社会における当該少数言語に対する評価についての認識が影響していると指摘している。すなわち、居住地の違いをも考慮に入れた視点が必要不可欠である。

　現在のところ、日本国外に居住する日本語と非英語の組み合わせの国際結婚家庭言語使用に関する研究[4]は非常に少ない。本研究は、二言語の組み合わせ、居住地の異なる多様な事例の一つとして、中国の北京在住日中国際結婚家庭を

---

[4] 上野（2014）と花井（2014）が韓国在住日本人母親と韓国人父親の家庭言語使用を、伊藤（2012）が台湾在住日本人母親と韓国人父親の家庭言語使用をそれぞれ異なる視点から研究報告している。

取り上げ、これらの家庭での言語使用の実態とそれに影響を及ぼす要因を質的に分析考察するものである。

近年、家庭で子どもの二言語を発達させるという目標に関連し、「家族言語政策」(Family Language Policy, 以下 FLP) という研究分野が注目されるようになってきた。本来国家で遂行される「言語計画」或いは「言語政策」の言語に対する選択の決定と遂行が、個人レベルの家庭でも行われると捉えたものである (King & Fogle, 2013; King, Fogle & Logan-Terry, 2008; Piller. 2001)。King, Fogle & Logan-Terry (2008) は、FLP はミクロレベルでの子どもの言語習得研究とマクロレベルでの言語政策研究を結び付けることで、複数言語家庭の言語使用に関する十全な理解を可能にすると指摘する。

言語政策から FLP を研究するものとして Spolsky (2009) がある。内部に独自の役割、関係があるそれぞれの領域に独自の言語政策があり、家庭は言語政策が行われる多様な領域の一つと捉える。その言語政策は相関しつつも独立した実践、信念、管理の3つの構成概念から成る (Spolsky, 2009, p. 4) とする。一方、言語習得から FLP を研究するものとして、家庭を言語社会化の重要な実践コミュニティとする立場 (Dōpke, 2008; Lanza, 2007) があり、家庭でのインタラクションが重視される。本研究では、インタラクション重視の立場を取り入れ、少数言語親と子どもの間でどのように少数言語が使用されているのかを親の家庭での役割という視点から捉える。したがって、研究課題を以下のように設定する。

(1) 対象家庭での言語使用は、どのように実践されているのか。
(2) 対象家庭での言語使用は、どのような信念のもとに実践されているのか。
(3) 対象家庭での言語使用は、どのように管理されているのか。
(4) 対象家庭で、少数言語話者である母親の役割はどのようなものか。

その上で、北京在住日中国際結婚家庭の言語使用について包括的な考察を行い、居住地の違い、二言語の組み合わせという点から、どのような特徴があるのかを探索する。

3. 調査方法及び調査対象

調査研究では、母集団を確定しランダムサンプリングを行うことが理想的であるが、個人的で散在する国際結婚家庭の母集団を掴むことは不可能であることから、一定の条件の下に仮の母集団を設定する。そこで、北京で1990年代半ばに設立された「中国人男性と結婚した日本人女性の会」(仮称N会) を仮の母集団とする。従って、家庭内での日本語母語話者はすべて母親である。

また、家庭内言語使用の変化を研究の焦点とするため、比較的長期間の過程を示すデータが必要となる。国際結婚家庭は移動性が高く、調査対象のN会会

員も子どもを連れて日本から中国へ移住したり、子どもが小さいうちに中国から日本や他の国・地域へ移住したりするケースが少なくない。そこで、社会主流言語を中国語とする環境で育った中学生以上の子ども[5]を持つ家庭を対象とし、把握できた全数データ[6]の収集に努めた。なお中学進学以降、転居や進学、留学等で中国語環境を離れ日本或いは他の国・地域へ移住した者を含み、その場合は移住前のデータを用いる。

具体的な調査方法は、条件に合致するN会の日本人母親28名に対して、半構造化面接調査を主とし、面接ができない5名はメールや電話で質問調査を行った。対象となった子どもについては、時間的制約や諸事情により、面接できたのは39名中19名である。調査は2013年から2015年にかけて数回に分けて実施し、録音されたものは文字起こしを行った。一人当たり1時間から5時間、親と子どものペアでの面接、親と子ども別々の面接、家庭によっては親のみ或いは子のみの面接、家族での面接等、それぞれの事情を考慮したため面接形態は多様である。面接はすべて日本語で、言語や生活にまつわるライフヒストリーを中心に行われた。

調査対象の母親の年齢は30代から50代、全員日本生まれの日本語母語話者、日本国籍者である。学歴は15名が四大卒以上、短大・専門学校卒が6名、大学中退1名、高卒2名、不明4名で、全体として高学歴である。1名を除き全員中国滞在は既に10年以上、長い者で20年を超え、中国語レベルは日常会話からビジネスレベルまで多様である。子ども39名については、大学生9名、高校生15名、中学生15名、中学までの在籍学校の形態は、日本人学校5名（うち3名は現地校と組み合わせ）、英語の国際校1名、英中バイリンガル校1名、その他は中国語を教授言語とする現地校である。性別は男22名、女17名である。

4. 調査結果

調査の結果、対象28家庭のうち、1家庭（事例26）の日本人母親が日本語を継承しないという選択をし、また1家庭（事例8）が家庭内で中国語を主として使用していた（既に日本へ移住）が、その他の家庭ではほぼ日本語が使用されていることが明らかになった。しかしその使用実態は、両親、子どもともに日本語を使用する家庭から、日本人母親が子どもに対して日本語と中国語を使い、子どもは母親に中国語で話すという家庭まであり、また兄弟間での言語も日本語、中国語、日本語と中国語と非常に多様で、話者の組み合わせごとに言語使用形態が変わるという点も、Yamamoto（2001a, 2001b）と同様の結果であった。表1はその結果をまとめたものである。プライバシーに配慮し、子ど

---

[5] 中島（2010）によると、年齢と第一言語/文化の習得の関係において、9〜10歳を境に言語形成期前半と後半に分けられる。後半では自立心が旺盛になり、自我に目覚め、勉強にも自分なりの取り組みができるようになるという。個人差を考慮して、一定レベルの言語形成が行われた中学生以上を調査対象とした。
[6] N会は名簿も会費徴収もない緩やかな団体であるため、全数は正確には掴めない。

もの年齢等家庭を識別できる情報を曖昧にしている。

表1. 家庭内話者間使用言語の状況（原則として 2015 年 8 月現在）

	子性別 注1	父/子 注2	母/子	兄弟	夫婦	言語使用形態 注3	母中国語力 注4	備考
1	m/m	J/J	J/J	J	J/J	少数	A	m_1 現地校→日本人学校　家政婦（C）
2	f	J/J	J/J	-	J/J	少数	A	日本人学校→現地校
3	f/m	C/C	J/J	J	C/C	OPOL	B	
4	m	J/J	J/J	-	J/J	少数	A	
5	m/f/f	C/C	J/J	JC	J/J	OPOL	A	兄妹間 J(mf_2) C(mf_1)(f_1f_2)
6	m/f	C/C	J/J	JC	C/C	OPOL	A	f 日本人学校 家政婦（C）
7	m	C/C	J/J	-	J/J	OPOL	A	
8	m/m	C/C	CJ/C	C	C/C	多数	C	日本→中国→日本
9	f/(m)	C/C	J/J	C	C/C	OPOL	C	祖母（C）
10	m/m	C/C	J/J	C	C/C	OPOL	B	
11	m/f	J/J	J/J	J	J/J	少数	A	f 混合（日中 8:2）
12	f	C/C	J/J	-	C/C	OPOL	B	
13	f	C/C	J/J	-	C/C	OPOL	B	祖父母（C）
14	f/m	C/C	J/J	C	C/C	OPOL	B	
15	f/m	C/C	J/JC	JC	C/C	OPOL	B	m 混合（日中 5:5）
16	m	C/C	J/J	-	J/J	OPOL	A	
17	m	C/C	J/J	-	C/C	OPOL	A	祖父（C）
18	m/(f)	C/C	J/J	JC	J/J	OPOL	B	
19	f/(m)	C/C	J/J	JC	C/C	OPOL	B	m_1 現地校→日本人学校→現地校
20	f	C/C	J/J	-	C/C	OPOL	B	
21	m	J/J	J/J	-	J/J	少数	A	英語国際校 家政婦（C）→中止
22	f/m/(m/m)	C/C	J/J	JC	J/J	OPOL	A	姉弟間 J(fm_1) C(fm_2m_3)($m_1m_2m_3$)
23	m/(f)	C/C	JC/JC	JC	C/C	混合	C	m 混合（中日 8:2）使用言語調整中
24	f	C/C	J/J	-	J/J	OPOL	A	

25	f/(m)	C/C	CJ/C	C	C/C	混合	A	F混合（中日 9;1）使用言語調整中
26	m	C/C	C/C	-	C/C	単一	C	
27	m/(f)	C/C	J/J	J	C/C	OPOL	A	日本人学校在籍
28	f	C/C	J/J	-	J/J	OPOL	A	英中バイリンガル校

注1：m, fはそれぞれ男、女を、m_1, m_2の数字は出生順を示す。（ ）は年齢上調査対象外の子どもである。
注2：C, Jはそれぞれ中国語、日本語を示す。
注3：後述の分類参照
注4：母親の中国語力を自己申請に基づき、（A）日常会話、（B）ビジネス、（C）ネイティブレベルで示す。

　以上の調査結果と面接調査の内容をもとに、対象家庭の家庭内言語使用について Spolsky（2009）の言語政策構成概念である言語の実践、信念、管理及び領域での役割という枠組みを用いて分析を行う。

5. 分析
5.1. 実践—家庭内言語使用の類型
　言語政策に関する実践は、観察可能な行為と選択であり、人々が実際に行っていること（Spolsky, 2009, p. 4）とされ、家庭領域での言語使用を指す。
　表1で示された家庭内の言語使用形態を、その特徴をもとにいくつかの型に分類した。家庭内で日本語を使用せず中国語のみである「単一言語」型、社会の多数派言語を主として使用する「多数言語」型、家庭内で日本語を使用する26家庭をさらに、日本語母語話者である母親が中国語と日本語を混合して使う「両言語混合」型、基本的にそれぞれの親が母語を使う家庭を「OPOL」型、両親ともに社会の少数派言語である日本語を使う家庭を「少数言語」型の5タイプに分け、それを表2にまとめた。

表2. 家庭内使用言語の類型

型	使用言語	特徴或いは事由	家庭数[注1]
単一言語	中国語のみ	日本語を継承しない	1(26)
多数言語	中国語が主	居住地の社会主流言語	1(8)
両言語混合	中国語と日本語の併存	母親の両言語混合使用	2(23,25)
一親一言語		基本的に OPOL	19
少数言語	日本語のみ	さまざま	5(1,2,4,11,21)

注1：括弧内は事例番号を表す。

　しかしながら、この類型は分析のための分類であり、面接調査の結果から、

少数言語型でも実際の生活では純粋に 100％日本語、OPOL 型でも一親 100％一言語であることは現実には難しいことが分かった。たとえ、「家庭ではすべて日本語です」という回答や、日本人母親の「私は子どもに日本語しか使いません」という自己申告があっても、細部について尋ねてみると、場面や話題、会話参加者によってコードスイッチングがあり、日本語使用にも中国語の単語やフレーズの無意識的な挿入があるのが一般的であった[7]。調査対象の家庭のほとんどが中国滞在 10 年以上であり、日本人母親の社会化が進行していることを考えると、当然の結果とも言える。そうした意味で、この 5 分類は分析のための大まかな枠組みとして考える。それぞれの型について分析は以下の通りである。

5.1.1. 単一言語型

調査対象のうち 1 家庭のみ、「複雑になるのは嫌だから、日本語の継承は行わない」という母親の信念のもと、家庭内言語を中国語に統一している。日本との行き来も少なく、日本との関わりは祖父母との交流に限定されている。この家庭では日本人母親のみがバイリンガルである。

5.1.2. 多数言語型

調査対象のうち 1 家庭のみ、日本では日本語、中国では中国語というように社会主流言語の多数派言語を家庭内主言語とした。「中国で 10 年、日本で 10 年生活し、子どもに両方の言語と文化を身に付けさせる」という現言語計画は、子どもの進路希望から日本再移住を決定した後に調整されたもので、最初からあったわけではない。日本へ再移住後 3 年経った現在、母親への子どもの言語は日本語にシフトし、父親とは中国語を使用、結果的に OPOL となっている。この戦略が有効であるためには、両親ともに日中バイリンガルである必要がある。

5.1.3. 両言語混合型

分析上の分類では現時点では 2 家庭のみである。事例 23 は上の子どもには当初 OPOL ではなく多数言語の中国語を家庭言語としたため、子どもの日本語使用が非常に制限されているケースである。事例 25 は上の子どもの現地幼稚園での適応を心配して、母親が中国語使用に切り替えた結果、子どもの使用言語が中国語にシフトしたケースである。両家庭とも父親は中国語モノリンガルで、母親は日中バイリンガルである。現在、母親は子どもへの日本語使用を増やすために OPOL 原則を採っている[8]。

---

[7] Kasuya（1998）でも、OPOL 使用を自己申告した親と子どもの実際の会話を観察してみると、二言語を混合していることを報告している。
[8] 表 1 は 2015 年 8 月現在のデータをもとにしているが、その後の変化については個別に報告を受けている。

5.1.4. 一親一言語（OPOL）型

19家庭がこの型に分類され、調査対象の多数を占める。しかし先に述べたように、一親が100%一言語を使用することは非現実的であり、厳密な意味のOPOL原則を採っている家庭は皆無と言ってよい。分類上の両言語混合型との違いは、親だけではなく子どもの言語使用にもある。換言すると、親が基本的にOPOLの言語使用をし、子どもも基本的に一親一言語の言語使用をしているかどうかである。但し、兄弟間で言語使用が分かれるケースがあり、事例15では姉は母親に日本語で会話するが、弟は日中半々であるという。この型では夫婦間の共通言語は必要であるが、両親のどちらも必ずしも日中バイリンガルである必要はない。

5.1.5. 少数言語型

家庭内言語を日本語に統一している5家庭すべて、日本から中国への移住組である。子どもを連れて日本から中国へ移住したのは10家庭（乳児期の移住は除く）であるが、日本居住時の家庭内言語使用は100%日本語であり、居住地による違いが明確である。中国移住後も引き続き家庭内言語が日本語である少数言語型をとったのは4家庭、OPOL型に切り替えたのが6家庭である。少数言語型のもう1家庭は乳児期の中国移住であったが、子どものバイリンガル教育を念頭に家庭言語政策として日本語を使うという言語選択を行っている。この型では父親が日中バイリンガルであることが必須条件となる。

以上のように、北京在住の母親が日本人である日中国際結婚家庭の家庭内言語使用では、厳密なOPOL原則ではなく、緩やかなOPOL型が主流を占めることが明らかになった。両言語混合型2家庭もまた、緩やかなOPOL型へ言語調整を行っている。そのプロセスはさまざまであるが、OPOL型が国際結婚家庭にとって、両親のバイリンガル能力を問わない最も自然で最も負担が少ない言語使用であることが示唆された。

5.2. 信念―言語イデオロギー

Spolsky（2009）による言語政策の2つ目の構成概念は言語や言語使用に関する信念であり、「言語イデオロギー」（King, Fogle, & Logan-Terry, 2008）や「信念と態度」（De Houwer, 1999）とも言われ、言語実践に大きな影響を与えるとされる。

調査の結果、中国人父親の子どもの言語についての考えは、単一言語型の家庭では不明であるのを除くと、すべての家庭で子どもがバイリンガル、マルチリンガルに育つことに肯定的であり、場合によっては非常に積極的であることが明らかになった。調査対象の28家庭中、父親が日本を含め外国に留学或いは就業経験がある者は19名、自らが海外業務に就くか仕事上外国との関わりがある者6名、外国との関わりは直接ないが海外在住の親族がいる者2名、結婚以外に全く外国と関わりがない者はわずか1名である。多くの父親が中国語と日

本語、或いは中国語とその他の言語のバイリンガルである[9]。

このように、バイリンガルに肯定的な中国語話者の父親の協力の下、家庭で少数言語を使用する主体である日本人母親は、どのような言語信念を持っているのだろうか。以下は、日本人母親が家庭内で子どもに日本語を使う動機について語ったものをカテゴリー化したものである。

5.2.1.「日本人」として継承する日本語

まず、非常に強い動機として、「日本人だから」[10]というものが挙げられる。この母の強い信念は相互作用の結果、子どももそれを受け社会化されていることが多い。こうしたケースはとりわけ日本で日本語を第一言語[11]として一程度習得した後に、中国へ移住した家庭に多く見られる。日本語と中国語を同時習得したケースでは、国籍としての日本と日本語を結び付けて語られた。

| 事例 1 | 「日本人として日本語を忘れてほしくない。将来日本に帰るであろうことを考え、きちんと習わせたい」。
| 事例 5 | （子ども第一子）「僕、日本人ですから」
| 事例 7 | 「『日本人って言われるなら、日本人である言葉を喋りなさい』って教えた」。
| 事例 13 | （子ども）「国籍日本を選んで、でも日本語できないっていうのは…」

そして、これらの母親が抱く「日本人」の概念には、言語だけでなく日本的価値観や習慣も含まれる。

| 事例 13 | （子どものマナー違反に対して）「『日本人なのに、日本のこと何も知らない』って、子どもに言う」。
| 事例 27 | 「子どもは日本人として育てたい」

5.2.2. コミュニケーションのための日本語

母親が母語でコミュニケーションをとる相手として、子どもの日本語習得を期待する動機も比較的多い。

| 事例 4 | 「日本語は母の存在の象徴なんです。そして、母と子をつなぐ大切なもの、子どもと一緒の時間なんです」。
| 事例 17 | 「自分が日本人だから日本語で話してほしいと思いますし、将来コ

---
[9] 中国語は方言が多いが、本稿では中国語とはマンダリン（普通話）を指す。父親の中で少数民族出身者が 1 名いるが、「一番使いやすいのは日本語」で、家庭内ではほぼ日本語である。
[10] 調査対象の子どもは、日本国籍者と日中二重国籍者が半々である。
[11] ここで言う「第一言語」は、生後初めて覚えた言語を指す。

ミュニケーションをとるときにも日本語で心を通わせたいと思って」。

事例20 「私は中国語あやしいんで、何かあったときに出るのはやっぱり日本語だから。私には日本語で話せる相手が欲しいなっていうのもあって」。

事例28 「この言葉の持つ意味を理解してほしい、フィルターを通さずにね。でも、あの子が理解してくれてるのは7割かなと思う、すごい寂しいけどね」。

そして、日本の祖父母とのコミュニケーションも子どもの日本語習得を願う理由の一つとなっている。

事例7 「（母親の）お父さんとお母さんと話ができないのは、（子どもと祖父母の）両方にとって可哀想だなって。せっかくの孫なのに中国だから日本語話せないからって言われたら、なんか私の選択間違ったかなみたいな、なっちゃうし、私の家族なのに子どもが「知らない人」みたいな、そう思われるのも嫌だったから、絶対話してほしかった」。

5.2.3. 子どもの将来への「投資」としての日本語

事例3 「私が子どもに確実に残せるのは日本語、中国語プラス日本語ができれば将来生活に困らないでしょう」。

事例17 「子どもが後悔しない選択をするための選択肢をいろいろ出してあげる、目の前に並べてあげるということはちゃんとしてあげないといけないかなと思って。やっぱり選択肢の中で可能性が高いとすれば日本語ですよね」。

5.2.4. バイリンガル育成のための日本語

事例18 「バイリンガル関係の本は買ったり借りたりしました。私の中で大きな軸となっているのは、『私は日本語だけを話す人でありたい』『できるだけ、私のゆがんだ中国語は子どもたちに学ばせてはいけない』『子どもたちは自分で中国語を矯正していけるように育てないといけない』、その部分ですかね」。

事例20 「友だちから一人一言語にした方がいいよって、経験者から。外国語を混ぜると子どもが混乱しちゃうから」。

しかしながら、以上の母親の言語信念がすべて子どもの誕生時からあったとは考えにくい。なぜならば、家庭内の言語選択を夫婦間の話し合いで決めたケースは少なく、多くは特別な話し合いもなく「自然に」「なんとなく」という回答であったからである。これらの信念は、子どもとのインタラクションや子どもの成長、外部環境との関係の過程で醸成されていったものではないかと考えら

れる。この点について、以下言語管理の観点からの分析が参考になると思われる。

5.3. 管理―家庭内言語使用の調整

Spolsky（2009）の言語政策の3つ目の要素は言語管理である。言語政策管理者が言語実践や信念を調整するために行う観察可能な明らかな取り組みであり、移住後の言語保持のための取り組み（Curdt-Christiansen, 2013）ともされる。言語管理として、子どもの少数言語発達を促進するために家庭内部に限らず外部の活動を通じて取り組みが行われているが、本項では特に家庭内言語調整の軌跡に焦点を当て分析を行う。

5.3.1. 日本から中国へ移住した家庭で、子どもの日本語力が落ちたと気づいたとき

家庭内外100%日本語であった日本での生活から中国移住後、引き続き家庭内言語を日本語とした家庭でも、中国語環境の現地幼稚園や小学校に通園通学する子どもの日本語力の衰えを何かのきっかけで感じると、母親は「もともとあった能力が衰退する」という不安に苛まれる。

> 事例1　*長男が小学校就学時に中国移住*
> 「子どもの日本語が日に日に落ちていくんですよ。日本語の補習校があればと思いましたが、北京にはなくて」（母親は日本語強化のための機会や環境を整える努力を行った）

子どもの中国語力を養うためOPOL型に移行した6家庭ではなおさらであったと思われる。

> 事例12　*一人娘が日本の幼稚園を卒園するのを待って中国移住*
> 「最初は娘の中国語を心配してたし、自分も中国語の勉強をしなきゃいけなくて余裕がありませんでした」「小学校4年生の頃、日本語がなんとなく落ちてきたなと感じたんです。いわゆる語順が狂ったり、『てにをは』がおかしくなった」「それで、ちょっと日本語テコ入れしなきゃと、児童向けの本を日本から取り寄せて、読み聞かせをしました。DSも買いました」「日本の小学校に体験入学もしました」

5.3.2. 父方親族に日本語使用を制限されたとき

多くの父親が子どものバイリンガル育成に理解があり協力的であるが、父方親族もそうであるとは限らず、2家庭が父方親族から家庭での日本語使用について明確に制限を受けた経験をもつ。

|事例 11| *子どもが6歳と3歳で中国移住、その直後父親の実家帰省時*
「『おまえ、子どもに向かって日本語しか話さないから、子どもの中国語が上手くいかないんだ！』『子どもとは中国語で喋れ！』って癇癪起こされたんですよ、舅に。ガ～ッと言われて私、しょげてたんですよ。その時、子どもたちが『ママは日本語の人！』『おかあさんは日本語を喋る人！』って言って、援護射撃が入ったんですよ。そうしたら舅、コロッと態度が変わんねん。（中略）だから私も子どもにはずっと日本語を喋ってるんです」

|事例 19| *父方親族が多い地方都市に住んでいた時*
「周りには、私が日本語を教えると混乱するからやめろって」「でも子どもが2才のとき、家族で乗ってたタクシーの中で流していた漫才を聞いて、私以外みんなでドッと笑い出したんですよ、娘も。それで『まずい』と。娘が分かるようなジョーク私分かんない。これから娘とコミュニケーションとっていけないと思って」（その後OPOL 型へ）

5.3.3. 多言語環境による影響に気づいたとき
|事例 21| *子どもが日本語をあまり喋らないため言語使用調整*
「英語の幼稚園に通っていて、英語と、家政婦さんがいたので中国語は入りやすくて。私と息子はずっと日本語で、主人とも家では日本語です。けれども、家政婦さんがいるとどうしても中国語で言っちゃうんですよ」「でもある日これじゃまずいと思って、家政婦さんを止めました。それから急に子どもの日本語が伸びましたね」

5.3.4. 兄弟間の会話が日本語から中国語にシフトしたとき
|事例 3| *母親が入院中に幼稚園児の姉弟間の会話が中国語にシフト*
「2か月の入院後、家に戻ってみたら、それまで日本語で会話をしていた姉と弟が中国語で話をしているのに驚きました。私がいないのだから当然と言えば当然なんですけど。それで、姉の方に「弟には日本語で話しなさい」と半ば強制しました。娘は最初嫌がりましたけど、このくらいの年齢だと戻るのも早かったです」

|事例 15| *姉が小学校入学後、姉弟間の会話に中国語*
「それまでほとんど日本語でした。姉が小学生になって中国語の言葉が増えると、弟がどんどん中国語を。でも、姉が日本語でパーッと喋ったら、弟は日本語で入っていきますね。半分くらいです。私は日本語で言いますね、弟に。そしたら日本語で返ってくる、でも中国語で返ってくる時もあるけど、私は努めて日本語にしています」（弟は高校進学後、日本のアニメへの関心から日本

語使用の比重が増加）

5.3.5. 第二子が生まれたとき

このケースは、両言語混合型の 2 家庭で明らかに見られた。両家庭の母親は異口同音に「上で失敗したから」と語り、OPOL アプローチに調整している（事例 23, 25）。また、現在 OPOL 型の家庭でも、第二子の誕生をきっかけにそれまでの混合型から調整を行った例もある（事例 3）。

5.3.6. 子どもの学業・進路問題に直面したとき

子どもの学業・進路問題は多くの家庭で最重要課題と位置づけられていることが明らかになった。いずれの場合も、進学を目指して日本語使用の強化がなされている。

> 事例 3　*早期に日本の大学進学を計画*
> 「父親が忙しく、子どもの教育は全部私に回ってきたんですよ。でも、日本人の私に中国人の親がやるような家庭教育はできないし、あんな受験競争にも参入したくない。で、子どもが小学生ぐらいの時、高校までは中国、大学を日本という計画を立てたんですよ。子どもがそれに乗るかどうかはともかく」。

> 事例 7　*中国の学校の寮生活に嫌気がさし、日本の高校進学へ*
> 「私には子どもの勉強が見れないので、子どもは小学校から中学校まで寮生活でした。週末と長期の休みに家に戻るのですけど、日本語はその時だけ。それでも私は中国語ができないので、母子の会話は日本語でした。高校進学を考えたときに、子ども本人が『寮はもう嫌だ』と言ったので、日本語のためにも日本の高校に進学するのがいいんじゃないかと考えました。それを決めてから、高校入試に合わせて日本語の作文指導を始めました」

5.3.7. 子どもの日本語の可能性を感じたとき

> 事例 17　*母の仕事の関係で母子別居、母子間言語が中国語になっていたが、日本に一時帰国時の体験から言語調整*
> （子どもが欲しかった iPad を母親に買ってもらえないと分かって）「そしたら母（子どもの祖母）のところに行って説得するんですよね。すごいなと思ったのは、日本語しか通じない人にはちゃんと日本語で説得するんですよ、iPad のために」、「私の母もちゃんと分かる日本語なんですよ。日本語こんなに上手かったんだって。クラスの皆持ってるとか、北京で買うとちょっと高いとかね、買ってほしい理由をちゃんと言えるんですよ」（その後、母親は OPOL に戻し、どんなに忙しくても年二度は子どもを連れて帰国した結果、母子間

の会話は日本語にシフトした）

　以上の語りから明らかなように、子どものバイリンガル発達は一様でもなく、直線的でもない。少数言語型でも、子どもが幼稚園で中国語を理解できないことを心配して一時期 OPOL を採用した少数言語型家庭（事例 4）、多数言語型で日本の学校へ進学のために OPOL を採用した家庭（事例 8）など、それぞれの家庭環境や条件の下で言語管理がなされ調整が行われている。こうした調整は、ある意味、家庭外部の影響に対する管理として、家庭言語使用に影響を与える正負の外部要因を特定する手がかりとなる。

5.4. 家庭内部の関係―日本人母親の家庭での役割
　少数言語に対する社会的サポートがない環境では、家庭での少数言語使用によって子どもの少数言語社会化が行われることから、家庭での少数言語のインタラクションのあり方、すなわち少数言語親と子どもの関係、或いは少数言語親の家庭での役割が重要な鍵となると思われる。

5.4.1. 少数言語話者としての役割
　事例20 「日本語喋るのは私しかいなかった」

5.4.2. 家庭内で父が学校教育、母が生活面という明確な役割分業
　事例 4 （子ども）「どっちかって言うと（生活面に関わる）母寄りなんで、親近感はありますね、（子どもの勉強や進路に関わる）父に比べて」
　事例 5 「父親が教育担当で、私が生活指導担当って分担ができてるんですよ」

5.4.3. 父親の家庭不在が多く、子どものことは母の責任
　事例 2 「父親が単身赴任の期間が長くて、あの子の話をする相手は私しかいないのよ。私しか窓口がないのよ」
　事例 7 「父親はいないことが多くて、出張とかで。だから私といる時間が長いんですよね。やっぱり言葉もちょっと女言葉っていうか。」「父親って、どこまで口出しするかですよね、もっと関わってほしいんですよね。でも『それは俺のやることじゃない』みたいな」
　事例14 「全部私任せなんですよ。勉強もそうだし、家庭教育みたいなのもそうだし、親みたいなのもそうだから」
　事例16 「子どもは父親とはあんまり。忙しいのであんまり時間がない。私とは学校の関係のことを話すことが多いです」

5.4.4. 日本語や日本文化への関心を子どもと共有する関係
　事例13 「子ども（高校生）が日本語の本を一緒に読もうとかね、言って来たりする、時々」

|事例 14|「ネットでバラエティとか一緒に見るじゃないですか、『これ見た、あれ見た』ってそういう内容も日本語でやりとりしてます」

5.4.5. 進路や将来について子どもの相談相手
|事例 11|「息子が日本の大学に行きたいって言いだして、パンフレット取り寄せたんですよ。見せたらそこがいいって。母子でネットのサイトを見たり、今度学校説明会にも行くんですよ、一緒に」
|事例 18|「主人は忙しいので、子どもの教育や進路については私が情報収集したり、相談に乗ることが多いです。高校進学のことで息子との話は増えたかもしれません」。

　調査対象の家庭では、少数例外（事例 17）を除いて、有職の母親であっても父親に比べて、子どもと過ごす時間が多いことが明らかになった。また多くの家庭で子育て、子どもの成長とともに教育や進路問題への対応が母親の役割となっていること、日本語や日本文化への関心を子どもと共有する役割も大きな特徴である。こうした家庭条件が母子関係の緊密化をもたらし、言語実践や信念を調整する言語管理が可能となっているのではないかと推察される。

6. 考察
6.1. 北京在住日中国際結婚家庭の言語使用
　中国人父親がバイリンガル環境に理解があるにせよ、中国語環境で少数言語の日本語を使用し、また子どもの日本語の習得を根気よく心がけていくには、日本人母親の強い信念や態度が欠かせない（De Houwer, 1999）。
　「日本人だから」、「母子のコミュニケーション」、「日本の祖父母との交流」、「子どもの将来」が、母親の日本語使用を支える信念であり、「日本の習慣や価値観を身に付けてほしい」という願いも生活面での日本語使用を促していると思われる。こうした日本語や日本文化の子どもへの継承は唯一日本人母親にかかっていることが、OPOL を基本とする言語使用を自然と導いているのではないかと思われる。また、母親の子育て、子どもの教育という家庭でのジェンダー的役割が言語使用に大きく影響していることが明らかになった。こうした母子のインタラクションを通じた心情的に緊な関係性が、インプットの量ではなく（事例 17）、コミュニケーション言語として子どもの日本語使用を促すのではないかと示唆された。移民家庭の母語継承に関する研究でも、家族の結びつき（Sakamoto, 2001）や家族の密接でフラットな関係（Tannenbaum & Howie, 2002）と母語保持の関連を指摘している。
　心情的に密な関係性とは、早期バイリンガル研究分野において、Döpke（2008）が指摘する「子ども中心性」（child-centeredness）が概念的に近いと思われる。子ども中心のインタラクションとは、子どもを会話に参加させるよう仕向けるような仕組みの会話であり、少数言語話者の親が子どもと一緒に遊ぶことが多

いと、子どもの少数言語発話を促すとされる (Lanza, 2007)。心情的に密な関係性は、子どもが成長し外部での社会化が進むと、「子どもの立場になって共感する」という形をとるようになると見られる。

| 事例16 | (教育方針について)「子どもに寄り添って、ですね」
| 事例17 | 「おじいちゃんとおとうさんからいろんなプレッシャーがあるので、ガス抜きをして、それが自分の役割かなと。子どもは同居のおじいちゃんとは事務的な話しかしません。おとうさんは勉強の話しかしないから、あまり話しないですね。(別居の) 私には『ママ、最近忙しいの』とか、割と心配してくれたり。私は子どもと本音で話しますから」

親がそれぞれの母語を使って子どもとインタラクションするOPOL概念に対し、子どもも親にそれぞれの親の母語を使ってインタラクションする双方向の言語使用を「双方向のOPOL」とし、その言語使用の実践と母子関係を母親の信念と家庭内役割との相互作用として、次の概念図で示したものである。この概念図では、言語管理はこれらに影響を与える言語調整として別次元のレベルのものと捉える。

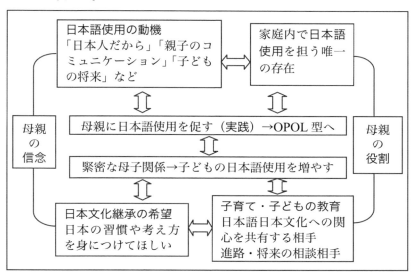

図1. 双方向の緩やかなOPOL型の概念図 (筆者作成)
注：矢印は相互作用を示す。

図1では、母親の日本語使用を促す信念と家庭内日本語話者が母親一人であるという少数言語話者としての役割が、緩やかなOPOLというコミュニケー

ションの原型を作り、日本文化継承の信念と家庭でのジェンダー的役割が、母子関係を緊密化し実質的なコミュニケーションを促進するということを視覚化している。このように、OPOL の緩い運用と母子関係のあり方が、北京在住日中国際結婚家庭の言語使用では、子どもの日本語使用を促す重要な要因であることが示唆される。

6.2. 二言語の組み合わせと居住地が家庭言語使用にもたらす影響

　調査の結果、北京在住日中国際結婚家庭では基本的にそれぞれの親が母語を使って子どもとコミュニケーションをする OPOL 型が圧倒的多数で、大半の子どもが日本人母親とのコミュニケーションに日本語を使用していることが確認された。これが、従来の OPOL 研究で見られる「OPOL は子どもの少数言語使用を必ずしも保証しない」(De Houwer, 2007; Yamamoto, 2001a: b) という結果と大きく異なることは明らかである。これが二言語の組み合わせ、居住地の違いとどう関わるのかについて、以下考察を行う。

　まず、二言語の組み合わせとして、社会の少数言語に対する評価という面から見ると、中国における日本語学習者は英語を除く外国語の中では最も多く、国際交流基金の 2012 年調査では約 105 万人が各種教育機関で日本を学習している。その背景には日中の経済関係や、それに関連した日本留学、日系企業への就職等の実利的ニーズに加え、日本のサブカルチャーや観光の面から日本文化への関心があると報告している[12]。したがって、中国での日本語の地位は決して低くはないと言える。調査対象の家庭でも、日本のサブカルチャーや日本での進学志望が日本語使用を増やしたのは、こうした社会的要因によるものと思われる。

　しかしながら、Yamamoto（2001a, 2001b）が、日本では英語のステータスが高いにも拘わらず、日英国際結婚家庭での OPOL が必ずしも子どもの英語使用をもたらさないことを指摘していることを考えると、本調査結果には他の要因が関わっていることが考えられる。英国在住日英国際結婚家庭の言語使用を家族関係や子育てとの関係を中心に調査した Okita（2001）の研究は、その研究の枠組みにおいて本研究に近く、両者を比較することによって調査対象者の居住地の違いによってもたらされる要因を見出すことを可能にすると思われる。まず Okita（2001）では、「コミュニケーション」を日本人母親の日本語使用の主たる動機とするが、本調査対象の母親においては「日本人」という面が非常に色濃い。そこには中国乃至は北京という独自の環境との相互作用があると考えられる。

　多民族国家である中国では民族の別が明確であり、国際結婚家庭であっても外国籍を持つ者は永遠に「同化」されない「外国人」である。北京では、「外国

---

[12] 国際交流基金各国の日本語教育事情（中国）2012 年調査 http://www.jpf.go.jp/j/project/japanese/survey/area/country/2014/china.html（2017 年 1 月 25 日アクセス）

人」¹³の子どもは就学や進学で他の子どもとは異なる待遇となる。また子どもが中国籍を持つ場合¹⁴であっても、学校での愛国主義教育や社会での反日ムードによって、母子ともども常に「日本人」を意識せざるを得ない状況が生み出されていることが明らかとなった。以下は、母親の一人が子どもの通う中学校で催された反日講演会に出席した時のことを綴った文章の一部である。

「私の右に座っている娘を見たかった。見守りたかったというか。でも、顔をそちらに向けられなかった。」「空気が凍てついた。私を包む空気だけが凍てついていた。娘にとっては初めてのことではない。」「このとき私が娘に顔を向けられなかったのは、申し訳なさから来ていた。私が国際結婚をしたから、相手が中国人だから。そして私が日本人で、生活の拠点が中国だから。娘がハーフだから。」「ふいに娘が小学 5 年生のときのことを思い出す。国語の教科書に『狼牙山五壮士』が紹介されていた。これも抗日英雄の話だ。『こういうふうに日本が教科書に出てきて、友達に何か言われないの』と聞いたとき、『いいの。無視するから』と娘は答えた。切なかった。それ以上何も言えなかった。」(みどり, 2013, p. 92-93)

中国社会の中で意識せざるを得ない「日本人」のラベルは、母子の間にある種の連帯意識を生み出し、それが心情的に緊密な母子関係とも結びついているのではないだろうか。同様に「日本の習慣や考え方」は中国との対比によって位置づけられる。しかし、岡崎 (2011) には、日本では子どもが「ハーフ」で目立つことを嫌がる母親と子どもの心理的なコンフリクトが指摘されていることから、北京でも「日本人」で目立つことを嫌い、N 会のネットワークに参加していない日中国際結婚家庭の日本人母親もいると想像される。したがって、本事例の調査の限界は否めない。

Okita (2001) の研究は本調査と同様に、本調査対象と同じ世代の家庭ではやはり父親の家庭不在が指摘されている。それは、異国で生活する母親は稼ぎ手の父親のような高収入の仕事を得ることが難しいため、母親が子育ての役割を担うという分業と、経済活況による父親の仕事の多忙、母親の子どもが小さいうちの子育てに関する信念などによる。中国の事例の多くも同じ解釈が可能であろう。それに加えて、配偶者の在留資格では就業が認められない法制度や「日本の習慣や考え方」継承の信念などが考えられる。

さらに、思春期の子どもに対する考え方に関して、中国の社会文化的要因による違いに注目する必要があろう。Okita (2001) では子どもの独立を促す「英国式」と子どもに関わる「日本式」の間での葛藤が報告されている。一人っ子家庭が大半である中国では、子ども中心の家族関係と緊密さ、儒教の伝統を背

---

[13] 中国の国籍法の運用は 2008 年頃を境に大きく変更され、それ以前は片親が中国人であっても外国で生まれた子どもは中国籍がないものと見なされた。
[14] 中国の国籍法は二重国籍を認めていないが、日本の国籍留保は黙認され、実質上二重国籍扱いとなっている。

景とした子どもへの教育投資が特徴的であり、相対的に自主独立的な「日本式」と子ども中心の「中国式」の間に葛藤があると思われる。中国における親が子どもに多く関わることを要請する社会文化は、家庭内での子育てや教育の役割と相まって、母子関係に影響を及ぼしているものと見られる。

以上のように、居住地である中国乃至は北京と英国の政治経済、社会文化的環境の違いが、家庭内の日本語と社会主流言語の家庭言語政策において我彼の差を生み出しているようである。そして、北京の事例から、エスニシティに支えられた強い言語信念と子育てを通した緊密な少数言語話者親と子どもの関係が、親と子の双方向の少数言語使用を促すのではないかという結論が導かれた。

最後に、言語学の観点から中国語と日本語の関係について見ると、言語系統が異なり音韻や文法の両言語間の距離は遠いため、音声言語には両言語の組み合わせによる有利な点はあまり考えられない。しかし表記媒体として共通の漢字を持つことが読み書きレベルでは有力な習得促進要素であることは疑いがない。したがって、日本語の読み書き習得によって、漢字の存在が本事例での言語使用に何らかの貢献をしていることが示唆される[15]。

7. おわりに

本稿では、北京在住の国際結婚家庭の言語使用について、家庭言語政策の枠組みを用いて分析考察を行った。その結果、多くの家庭で OPOL に近い言語使用が見られ、OPOL の緩やかな運用が最も自然で最も負担が少ないものとして受け入れられていることが明らかになった。また少数言語のインプット量の多寡よりも、母子の心情的に緊密な関係性が、コミュニケーションの中で子どもの日本語使用を促すということが示唆された。本研究の結果をそのまま一般化はできないが、言語の組み合わせや居住地の異なる研究によって、新たな視点を見出す可能性が示されたと言える。したがって、今後より多様な地域の多くの事例、そして逆の国際結婚の組み合わせについても研究がなされることが望まれる。

参照文献

伊藤佳代（2012）.「在台日台国際結婚家庭子女の日本語能力保持・伸長に関わる要因について―日常的な日本語言語活動を中心に―」『台大日本語文研究』23: 185-214.

上野由香子（2014）.「韓日国際結婚家庭の使用言語とその決定要因―言語環境と二言語環境に分ける家庭的要因を中心に―」『日本語文学』第 61 輯: 95-118.

---

[15] 柳瀬（2017）は、漢字の同根語が現地校で先行学習した中国語から日本語への言語間転移を促し、家庭で日本語を継承する子どもの漢字を含む日本語語彙習得を促進させると主張している。

岡崎ラフ和子（2011）．「バイリンガル教育に関わる3つの心理社会的要因」『大阪工業大学紀要人文社会篇』55(2): 29–38.

中島和子（2010）．『マルチリンガル教育への招待―言語資源としての外国人・日本人年少者』東京：ひつじ書房．

花井理香（2014）．「国際結婚家庭の言語選択と社会的要因―韓日国際結婚家庭の日本語の継承を中心として―」『異文化間教育』39: 51–64.

みどり（2013）．「娘が体験した気まずさを知る」在中日本人108人プロジェクト（編）『在中日本人108人のそれでも私たちが中国に住む理由』阪急コミュニケーションズ，pp. 90–93.

柳瀬千惠美（2017）．「中国における継承日本語学習者の漢字習得―同根語による言語間転移に着目して―」『MHB研究』13: 70–91.

Curdt-Christiansen, X. L. (2013). Family language policy: Sociopolitical reality versus linguistic continuity. *Language Policy, 12,* 1–6.

De Houwer, A. (1999). Environmental factors in early bilingual development: The role of parental beliefs and attitudes. In G. Extra & L. Verhoeven (Eds), *Bilingualism and migration* (pp. 75–96). Berlin: Mouton de Gruyter.

De Houwer, A. (2007). Parental language input patterns and children's bilingual use. *Applied Psycholinguistics, 28*(3), 411–424.

Döpke, S. (1998). Can the principle of the 'one person-one language' be disregarded as unrealistically elitist? *Australian Review of Applied Linguistics, 21*(1), 41–56.

Genesee, F. (2006). Bilingual first language acquisition in perspective. *Childhood bilingualism: Research on infancy through school age,* 45–67.

Kasuya, H. (1998). Determination of language choice in bilingual children: The role of input. *International Journal of Bilingualism, 2*(3), 327–346.

King, K. A. & Fogle, L. W. (2013). Family language policy and bilingual parenting. *Language Teaching, 46*(2), 172–194.

King, K. A., Fogle, L., & Logan-Terry, A. (2008). Family language policy. *Language and Linguistics Compass, 2*(5), 907–922.

Lanza, E. (2007). Multilingualism and the family. In P. Auer & W. Li (Eds.), *Handbook of multilingualism and multilingual communication* (pp. 45–67). Berlin/New York: Mouton de Gruyter.

Okita, T. (2001). *Invisible work: Bilingualism, language choice and childrearing in intermarried families.* Amsterdam, The Netherlands: John Benjamins.

Palviainen, Å. & Boyd, S. (2013). Unity in discourse, diversity in practice: The one person one language policy in bilingual families. In M. Schwartz & A. Verschik (Eds.), *Successful family language policy: Parents, children and educators in interaction* (pp. 223–248). Dordrecht: Springer.

Piller, I. (2001). Private language planning: The best of both worlds? *Estudios de Sociolinguistica, 2*(1), 61–80.

Sakamoto, M. (2001). Exploring societal support for L2 learning and L1

maintenance: A socio-cultural perspective. *Australian Review of Applied Linguistics, 24*(2), 43–60.
Spolsky, B. (2009). *Language management.* Cambridge: Cambridge University Press.
Tannenbaum, M. & Howie, P. (2002). The association between language maintenance and family relations: Chinese immigrant children in Australia. *Journal of Multilingual and Multicultural Development, 23*(5), 408–424.
Yamamoto, M. (2001a). *Language use in interlingual families: A Japanese-English sociolinguistic study.* Clevedon: Multilingual Matters.
Yamamoto, M. (2001b). Does the "one parent-one language" principle work? *Educational Studies, 43*, 235–240.
Yamamoto, M. (2002). Language use in families with parents of different Native languages: An investigation of Japanese-non-English and Japanese-English families. *Journal of Multilingual and Multicultural Development, 23*(6), 531–554.
Yamamoto, M. (2005). What makes who choose what languages to whom?: Language use in Japanese-Filipino interlingual families in Japan. *The International Journal of Bilingual Education and Bilingualism, 8*(6), 588–606.
Yamamoto, M. (2008). Language use in interlingual families: Do different languages make a difference? *International Journal of Soc. Lang., 189*, 133–148.

An exploratory study on the language use at home in Japanese-Chinese intermarried families in Beijing: Within the framework of Family Language Policy

Chiemi YANASE, Kyushu University

Abstract

There is a belief known as the "one parent-one language" principle, a way in which parents each consistently speak their first language to their child in intercultural families. The aim of this paper is to explore how parental languages are actually used at home in specific settings such as Japanese-Chinese intermarried families in Beijing, and to illuminate the relationships among linguistic practices, beliefs, management, and the role of the minority language-speaking parent in the family domain, within the framework of Family Language Policy (FLP). The research focuses on 28 Japanese-Chinese families in Beijing, of which the mothers are all native Japanese speakers. Through the interviews, it was clarified that the "one parent-one language" principle had been adopted flexibly in time and space, and most of the children used Japanese with their mothers in their families. The analyses demonstrated that such bi-directional minority language use between a mother and her child interrelates with her strong beliefs concerning the language and her role in the family. Furthermore, the study shows that an intimate relationship between the minority language-speaking parent and child is crucial for children's use of the minority language.

Deictic expressions in L2 narratives in Japanese: The case of demonstratives and donatory verbs

Noriko YABUKI-SOH, York University

Abstract

This study examined the use of deictic expressions found in the written narratives of second language (L2) learners of Japanese. It focused on two types of deixis in L2 learners' writing that were compared with those of Japanese native speakers: the demonstratives *kore/kono* "this" and *sore/sono* "that," and the donatory verbs *ageru, kureru* "give" and *morau* "receive," as well as their auxiliary verbs. The purpose of this investigation was to determine the cause of L2 learners' insufficient or inappropriate use of Japanese deixis when they described stories that involved multiple characters. The results suggested that (1) L2 learners' use of demonstratives was limited to *sono* + noun that referred to the main character of each story, and (2) learners tended to choose expressions of giving and receiving based on the characters that initiated an action in the story, causing a shift in viewpoint in the narratives. It would be beneficial for L2 learners to be aware of the anaphoric use of demonstratives and to pay attention to viewpoint when choosing donatory verbs in their narratives.

1. Introduction

Deixis refers to words and phrases that cannot be fully understood without contextual information. For instance, *I* and *you* are examples of personal deixis, *here* and *there* are instances of place deixis, and expressions such as *yesterday* and *today* denote temporal deixis: these words all require contextual information in order for the interlocutors to have a mutual understanding of what they actually refer to. Fillmore (1997) describes deixis as aspects of language that "can be interpreted only when the sentences in which they occur are understood as being anchored in some social context, that context defined in such a way as to identify the participants in the communication act, their location in space, and the time during which the communication act is performed" (p. 59).

Japanese is often considered to be a subjectivity-prominent language. Iwasaki (1993) investigated grammatical phenomena related to the speaker's perspective, and stated that in Japanese discourse, the existence of the speaker is distinctly reflected in various lexical and morphosyntactic outlets, including deictic verbs in Japanese. Ikegami (2005) observes that "Japanese belongs to the type of language in which the 'ego'/'alter' contrast plays a relatively prominent role" (p. 138). Ikegami (1989) further suggests that it is a unique aspect of the Japanese language that the speaker's viewpoint is encoded at the morphological and syntactic levels, in which linguistic devices such as the passive form of verbs or deictic expressions that include giving/receiving verbs and motion verbs (e.g., *iku* "go" and *kuru* "come") are often employed.

Japanese demonstrative words (i.e., *ko-so-a-do* words) and verbs of giving and receiving (e.g., *ageru*, *kureru* "give" and *morau* "receive") are two areas in which the notion of deixis is especially significant. The use of such deictic expressions is highly context-dependent, and it is closely associated with the concept of viewpoint in Japanese. Although second language (L2) learners of Japanese may have knowledge of deictic expressions, insufficient or inappropriate use of them is often observed in their written production. It is therefore pedagogically important to determine the differences in the use of deixis between L2 learners and native speakers of Japanese in order to promote L2 learners' acquisition of Japanese deictic expressions.

2. Deictic expressions in Japanese
2.1. Demonstratives

Similar to the English demonstratives "this" and "that," the triple system of Japanese *ko-so-a* words has both non-anaphoric and anaphoric usages. The *ko*-series, *so*-series, and *a*-series can refer to something visible that is near the speaker, near the hearer, and at a distance from both the speaker and the hearer, respectively. Those demonstratives can also be used anaphorically to refer to something that the speaker or the hearer has mentioned. According to Anderson and Keenan's (1985) classification, though, Japanese is a language that employs a "person-oriented system" in which the *ko-so-a* words are contrasted as first-person oriented, second-person oriented, and third-person oriented, as opposed to a "distance-oriented system" in which demonstratives can be contrasted in terms of the distance from the speaker. Ikegami (2005) adapts Shoho's (1981) analysis in which the *ko-so-a* words are viewed as comprising the "contrast type," where the speaker and the hearer are contrasted with each other and the *ko*- and *so*-words are used contrastively, and the "merger type" where the hearer is merged with the speaker in the use of the *ko*- and *a*-words. Ikegami replaces the notions of speaker and hearer with "ego" and "alter ego," and suggests that in either type of situation, "ego" plays an important role.

Kinsui and Takubo (1990) further analyzed the non-anaphoric and anaphoric uses of demonstratives in Japanese based on a perspective of discourse management. The non-anaphoric use implies a situation where a noun phrase with a demonstrative refers to someone or something that is present in the physical environment, and the anaphoric use indicates a situation in which a cohesive relation between a noun phrase with a demonstrative and its antecedent is established in the discourse. Kinsui and Takubo characterized the Japanese *ko-so-a* words as proximal-neutral-distal, respectively, based on the notion of psychological distance between the speaker and the referent. They suggested that the *so*-series is the unmarked demonstrative whereas the *ko*-series requires the speaker's special motivation such as emphasis, and that the *so*-series is used to indicate referents that are not found in the shared knowledge between the speaker and hearer, and therefore is the neutral form of anaphoric demonstratives.

2.2. Donatory verbs

There are three alternative ways to describe an event where the ownership of a book moves from person A to person B when using the informal forms[1] of verbs in Japanese: A *wa/ga* B *ni hon o ageta/yatta*, A *wa/ga* B *ni hon o kureta* "A gave B a book," and B *wa/ga* A *ni hon o moratta* "B received a book from A." The first two sentences use the giving verbs *ageru/yaru* and *kureru*, and share the same topic or subject, person A, who is the agent of an action of giving. In the first sentence, however, the event is described either from a neutral or person A's (the giver's) viewpoint, whereas in the second sentence, the same event is described from person B's (the receiver's) viewpoint. In the third sentence, the topic or subject of the sentence is person B, and the given event is also described from B's viewpoint. The auxiliary forms such as Verb-*te yaru/ageru* and Verb-*te morau* are used to describe the giving and receiving of favourable actions, and these devices[2] can also be regarded as the indicators of narrative viewpoints.

In explaining the notion of "empathy" that is defined as the speaker's identification with a person or thing that is being described, Kuno (e.g., 1978a, 1987) uses the metaphor of a camera angle that directors would use to decide what to focus on when filming a scene. Kuno (1987) observes that Japanese is "a language which has a built-in mechanism for overtly specifying what the speaker's camera angle is" (p. 245) and refers to the use of giving verbs such as *yaru* and *kureru* as an example of the use of such a mechanism. These verbs both represent an action of giving but indicate different viewpoints. Ikegami (2005), on the other hand, sees a parallel between the Japanese verbs *kureru/ageru* "give" and *kuru/iku* "come"/"go." He suggests that when one uses *kureru*, the sentence means that the gift "comes" to "ego," whereas a sentence with *ageru* means the gift "goes" to "alter." Thus, expressions that include Japanese donatory verbs such as *ageru*, *kureru*, and *morau* are closely related to what viewpoint the speaker takes in discourse.

---

[1] Kuno (1987) treats *yaru/kureru* as informal forms, *ageru* as a semi-honorific form, and *sashiageru/kudasaru* as honorific forms of giving verbs.

[2] Among the three auxiliaries (V-*te yaru/ageru*, V-*te kureru*, and V-*te morau*), V-*te yaru/ageru* is considered to put the viewpoint on the subject of the sentence, whereas the bare verb *yaru/ageru* indicates a neutral viewpoint as well (Kuno, 1978b).

2.3. Previous research

Few studies have compared the use of specific deictic expressions between first language (L1) and L2 narratives in Japanese. For instance, Watanabe (2012a) analyzed the prenominal demonstratives *kono* "this" and *sono* "that" in storytelling compositions produced by native speakers and L2 learners (L1: English) of Japanese. The results indicated that the native speakers used a small number of *sono* + noun phrases mainly to refer to people, things, and places that are newly introduced in the story, while L2 learners produced many more *sono* + noun phrases than native speakers did but mostly to refer to people in the story. These results also supported part of the findings of Watanabe's (2010) earlier study, which compared the use of the Japanese demonstratives *kono* and *sono* and that of the English prenominal demonstratives "this" and "that" found in the L1 Japanese and L1 English written narratives. According to Watanabe, while the unmarked demonstrative was found to be *sono* in the Japanese data, it was the demonstrative "this" in the English data. The results also indicated that although prenominal demonstratives in both languages function to indicate whether or not a referent is important, *sono* + noun was used to mark less important characters and objects, while English "this" + noun was used to mark more important characters and objects in the story.

As for donatory expressions, Okugawa (2007) compared the use of giving/receiving auxiliary verbs (e.g., V-*te ageru* "do a favour of V-ing") produced by native speakers and L2 learners of Japanese in their written narratives as part of her investigation on viewpoint and cognitive construal in storytelling discourse. She reported that native speakers almost always fixed the viewpoint on the main character when using the giving/receiving auxiliary, while L2 learners did not fix the viewpoint on any specific character in their narratives and often used the auxiliary verb V-*te ageru* where V-*te kureru* would be considered more appropriate in the discourse. Watanabe (2012b) further examined the use of perspective expressions (e.g., verbs in the passive form and giving/receiving expressions) in the written narratives of native speakers and L2 learners of Japanese. In this study, half of the L2 participants were given instruction on perspective expressions prior to the writing task and were also instructed to write the compositions from the main character's viewpoint. The results indicated that native speakers employed perspective expressions to maintain the main character's viewpoint, while L2 learners without instruction tended to shift the viewpoint from character to character. Watanabe's results also showed that L2 learners who had received instruction tended to overuse the passive forms of verbs instead of using V-*te morau* "receive a favour of V-ing." Nakahama and Kurihara (2007), on the other hand, compared the use of giving/receiving expressions among others (e.g., motion verbs, voice, and emotive expressions) that are related to narrative viewpoint between L1 and L2 Japanese in storytelling compositions. Their results on the count of those expressions showed that native speakers tended to set the viewpoint on one of the two given characters, while most of the L2 learners placed the viewpoint on both characters. Their findings also suggested that native speakers who chose related expressions to shift the viewpoint to the other character had inserted a conversational or inner speech, and employed emotive expressions at the end of the story in order to smooth the shift and maintain the viewpoint on a single character. L2 learners, however, tended to shift the viewpoint between the two characters across the different episodes in the story.

All of the above-mentioned studies suggest that there are functional differences between L1 and L2 narratives in the use of Japanese deixis. Watanabe's and Okugawa's studies, however, were conducted on data collected from compositions that described an animated story — the story was not designed to elicit specific deictic expressions. The pictures used by Nakahama and Kurihara, on the other hand, involved only two characters with equal importance in the story.[3] Details of what kind of deixis is chosen by L2 learners when describing specific stories with multiple characters that provide different viewpoint settings are still unknown. Further research that employs a tailored elicitation instrument is needed in order to shed more light on L2 learners' use of those deictic expressions in Japanese.

3. The study
3.1. Research questions

Based on the research discussed above, the present study attempted to further explore L2 learners' use of Japanese deixis in written narratives. The study investigated how the learners as narrators chose demonstratives and donatory verbs in their description of events in the stories, and how those expressions functioned in the narratives. The purpose of this investigation was to determine the cause of L2 learners' insufficient or inappropriate use of deictic expressions. Following are the research questions that guided the investigation:

1. What are the differences in the frequency and types of the Japanese demonstrative words *kore/kono* and *sore/sono* between L2 learners' narratives and those of native speakers?
2. What are the differences in the frequency and functional use of the Japanese donatory verbs *ageru*, *kureru*, and *morau*, as well as the auxiliary verbs V-*te ageru*, V-*te kureru*, and V-*te morau* between L2 learners' narratives and those of native speakers?
3. What are the possible causes of those differences, and what can be done to improve L2 learners' use of these deictic expressions?

---

[3] In Nakahama and Kurihara (2007), it was the authors' intention to let the writers decide which of the two characters to focus on when describing the given story.

3.2. Participants and data collection

The participants in the study were 16 L2 learners of Japanese who had completed university Japanese language courses at the intermediate and advanced levels, and 16 native speakers of Japanese. The L2 learners' L1 was English. L2 participants were selected based on a questionnaire that was used to determine their language background (English as their "most fluent language now"), their overall course grade (B+ or higher), and the results of a multiple-choice test that included some questions on Japanese demonstratives and donatory verbs, among others (90% or higher). This test was conducted to ensure that the L2 learners had sufficient knowledge of those deictic expressions at the time of their participation. Native speakers were mainly exchange students from Japan.

All of the participants wrote, in Japanese, descriptions of the four cartoon strips that are shown in the Appendix. Each of the cartoons consisted of four panels, and each story included activities of the giving and receiving of things (cartoons #1 and #2) or favours (cartoons #3 and #4) taking place between the given characters. In each story there was a main character, the boy in shorts, who appeared in all of the panels (participants were notified that he was the main character), and one to three other characters that were involved in the giving and receiving activities. Participants were instructed to describe the content of each cartoon so that someone who had not seen it would understand the story. L2 learners were allowed to consult a dictionary. In total, 128 short compositions were collected from the L2 learners and native speakers. The length of each composition varied among participants and across the four cartoons, but the average number of sentences and phrases used in the compositions was about the same between L2 learners (7.2 sentences per story and 13.5 phrases per sentence) and native speakers (6.3 sentences per story and 18.3 phrases per sentence).

All of the declarative sentences or clauses[4] (e.g., relative clauses and subordinate clauses) that included demonstrative words and donatory verbs/auxiliary verbs or their equivalent were first extracted. The use of demonstratives and donatory expressions was then compared in its frequency and type between the L2 learners and native speakers (marked as L2Ls and NSs, respectively, in the tables and exemplar sentences in the following sections).

3.3. Results
3.3.1. Demonstratives *kore/kono* and *sore/sono*

Table 1 shows the results for the number of the demonstratives *kore/kono* and

---

[4] In this paper, the term "phrase" is used as the smallest unit of constituent (e.g., a noun with a case marker), whereas "clause" is used to describe a syntactic construction that involves clausal modification or subordination.

sore/sono used in the 128 compositions.

Table 1. Demonstratives used in narratives: Cartoons #1–#4

	ko-series		*so*-series		Total
	kore	*kono* + noun	*sore*	*sono* + noun	
L2Ls (n=16)	1	4	5	23	33
NSs (n=16)	2	3	25	52	82

The overall results indicated that native speakers used demonstrative words much more frequently (an average of 5.1 times per person) than L2 learners (an average of 2.1 times per person). This result is different from that of Watanabe (2012a), in which he reported that non-native speakers of Japanese produced many more instances of *sono* than native speakers did. The method of data collection (i.e., oral versus written) or the types of characters and things that appeared in the stories[5] could be the possible cause of differences between the two studies in the overall frequency of demonstratives.

Regarding the *ko*-series, *kore* and *kono* were used a small number of times by the L2 learners and native speakers to begin their stories (four and three instances, respectively), as in *Kore wa ... no hanashi desu* "This is a story about ... ," and *Kono hanashi wa ...* "This story is ... ." The *ko*-series was also used by the L2 learners and native speakers (two and one instances, respectively) as in *Kono oishisōna ringo wa ...* "This delicious-looking apple is ... ," in which *kono* appears to be employed "semianaphorically as if the object being talked about were visible and were at the speaker's side" (Kuno, 1978a, p. 290). No other types of *kore* or *kono* were observed in the narratives.

The *so*-series was used much more often than the *ko*-series both by L2 learners (28 versus five instances, respectively) and by native speakers (77 versus five instances, respectively). All of the instances of *sono* + noun[6] were used with definite noun phrases that had antecedents as described in (1), in which *sono ringo* ("that apple," marked as "(ii)") matches its antecedent *ringo* ("apple," marked as "(i)").

(1) *Onna no ko ga ringo*[(i)] *o tabete imasu. Sono ringo*[(ii)] *wa ...*
    "A girl is eating an apple. That apple is ... "   (NS-01)

The overall frequency of the *so*-series found in the L2 learners' narratives was

---

[5] For instance, Watanabe (2012a) used a video clip from "Pingu," a children's animated cartoon. Pingu is the name of the main character, an anthropomorphized penguin, whereas the cartoon strip used in the present study had a generic set of characters with no proper names, including the main character.
[6] Formulaic uses of *sono* as in *sono ato* "and then" were not included in the results.

lower (an average of 1.8 times per person) than that in the native speakers' narratives (an average of 4.8 times per person).

Of the *so*-series, the differences between the written narratives produced by the L2 learners and native speakers were mainly found in the functional use of the demonstrative *sore* as a pronoun and the prenominal demonstrative *sono* + noun. Parts of the descriptions of cartoon #1 written by a L2 learner and a native speaker are shown in (2) and (3), respectively.

(2) *Okāsan wa imōto ni fūsen o yarimashita. Imōto wa ureshikute, onīsan ni fūsen o agemashita.*
"The mother gave a balloon to the sister. The sister was happy and gave (the) balloon to her brother. (L2L-03)

(3) *Imōto wa okāsan kara ōkii fūsen o moraimashita ga, otoko no ko ni orei to shite <u>sono</u> fūsen o purezento-shimashita.*
"The sister got a big balloon from their mother, but (she) gave the balloon to the boy as a present." (NS-03)

The noun *fūsen* "balloon" appears twice in both (2) and (3), but in (2), both are used with no demonstratives while in (3), the second *fūsen* is modified by *sono*. Without the use of the definite noun phrase *sono fūsen* "that balloon" as shown in (2), sentences produced by L2 learners were somehow difficult to follow. In contrast, in describing this same part of the cartoon, 11 out of 16 native speakers used *sono fūsen* "that balloon" in their sentences, as shown in (3).

Other examples of instances of *sono* produced by a L2 learner and a native speaker are presented in (4) and (5), respectively.

(4) <u>Sono</u> *otoko no ko wa obāsan o tetsudaitai to omotta. Sorede,* <u>sono</u> *otoko no ko wa obāsan no hō ni te o sashidashita.*
"The boy thought he wanted to help the old woman. So, the boy reached his hand out toward the old woman." (L2L-08)

(5) *Otoko no ko wa obāsan o tasukeyō to shita. Shikashi,* <u>sono</u> *obāsan ni gyakuni tasukerarete ōdanhodō o wataru koto ni natte shimatta.*
"The boy tried to help the old woman. However, (he) ended up crossing the crosswalk, being helped by the old woman instead." (NS-11)

In (4), the demonstrative *sono* modifies *otoko no ko* "boy," the main character of the story, and the noun phrase functions as a subject in each of the sentences. In (5), *sono* modifies *obāsan* "old woman," a secondary character that has just been introduced in the story, and the noun phrase is used as part of a subordinate clause of the sentence: this indicates that *sono* + noun was used to mark a less important character. It is noteworthy that in these examples the L2 learner repeatedly produced *sono* + noun together with the topic marker *wa* to refer to the already introduced main character, whereas the native speaker used topic omission in referring to the main character. Overall, L2 learners tended to use the prenominal demonstrative *sono* with the main character as a referent (14 out of 23 instances of *sono* + noun), whereas native speakers used *sono* when referring to a subsequently introduced secondary character, thing, or event (41 out of 52 instances of *sono* + noun). This finding is consistent with that of Watanabe (2012a). A chi-squared test reveals that there was a statistically significant difference between the L2 learners and native speakers in their use of *sono* for the main character and a secondary character, thing, or event ($\chi^2(1)=11.32, p<.01$).

In order to further examine the functions of the *so*-series used by the participants, the referents of the demonstratives *sore* and *sono* + noun were categorized as *koto* "event," *hito* "person," and *mono* "thing," according to what they refer to in the narratives. Table 2 shows the results of this categorization.[7]

Table 2. Referents of the *so*-series demonstratives used in narratives

	koto "event"		*hito* "person"		*mono* "thing"	
	sore	*sono* + noun	*sore*	*sono* + noun	*sore*	*sono* + noun
L2Ls (n=16)	2 (7%)	2 (7%)	—	19 (68%)	3 (11%)	2 (7%)
NSs (n=16)	22 (29%)	16 (21%)	—	15 (19%)	3 (4%)	21 (27%)

The results indicate that L2 learners in this study mainly used the *so*-series to refer to people (68%), whereas native speakers used *sore* and *sono* + noun more often to refer to events (50%) or things (31%). The counts produced by the two groups were statistically significant in their use of the *so*-series for "people" and "events" ($\chi^2(1)=19.13, p<.01$), as well as for "people" and "things" ($\chi^2(1)=9.91, p<.01$). As indicated earlier, most of the instances that count "people" as the referent of the demonstratives in the L2 narratives were the main character, while native speakers used those demonstratives to refer to subsequently introduced secondary characters in their narratives.

Another major difference in the use of demonstratives observed between L1 and L2 narratives is that among the *so*-series that refers to *koto* "event," native speakers often used *sore* or a *sono* noun phrase within a relative clause, as shown in (6) and (7).

---

[7] A small number of occurrences of *soko* "that place" (three and nine instances produced by L2 learners and native speakers, respectively) was also observed.

(6) *Onna no ko ga ōkina ringo o tabete ita. Sore o mita otoko no ko wa onna no ko ni hanashikaketa.*
"A girl was eating a big apple. A boy, who saw that, talked to the girl."
(NS-02)

(7) *Onna no ko ga ojīsan ga michi o wataru no o tetsudatte imasu. Sono kōkei o mita otoko no ko wa ...*
"A girl is helping an old man cross the street. A boy, who saw that scene, ..."
(NS-15)

In the second sentence in (6), a non-restrictive relative clause *sore o mita otoko no ko* "a boy who saw that" is used to describe a causal relationship between two sequential events (i.e., "seeing that" and "talking to the girl"),[8] in which *sore* is functioning as a demonstrative that refers to the content of the previous sentence. Similarly in (7), the prenominal *sono* in the second sentence is used to refer to the scene described in the first sentence. This type of *so*-series within a relative clause was employed by 11 out of 16 native speakers in one or more compositions, but the same type was not observed in L2 narratives.

3.3.2. Donatory verbs and auxiliaries

Table 3 presents the results for the number of different donatory expressions[9] that were used to describe the stories of cartoons #1 and #2, in which the characters give and receive things. In Tables 3 and 4, the arrows indicate the direction of giving/receiving activities (if the subject of a sentence is omitted, it was inferred based on the verb), and the characters[10] on which the viewpoint is based are emphasized in bold letters.

Table 3. Donatory expressions used in narratives: Cartoons #1 and #2

#		Structure with *ageru/yaru, kureru,* or *morau*	L2Ls (n=16)	NSs (n=16)
1	Boy → Sister	**Boy** *ga/wa* Sister *ni ageru*	13	15
		Sister *ga/wa* Boy *ni morau*	2	0
		others	1	1
	Mother	**Mother** *ga/wa* Sister *ni ageru/yaru*	9	3

---

[8] Masuda (2001) considers this type to be a relative clause with a discourse-level function (*danwa tenkai-gata rentaisetsu*).
[9] Some participants referred to the same donatory event more than once in their compositions. Part of the total number of expressions in Tables 3 and 4, therefore, exceeds the total number of participants (16 in each group).
[10] Different words were occasionally used by participants to address each character (e.g., *otoko no ko* and *shōnen* for the boy, *obāsan* and *rōjin* for the old woman).

	→ Sister	Mother *ga/wa* **Sister** *ni kureru*	4	6
		Sister *ga/wa* Mother *ni morau*	2	7
		others	1	0
	Sister → Boy	**Sister** *ga/wa* Boy *ni ageru*	10	4
		Sister *ga/wa* **Boy** *ni kureru*	2	6
		Boy *ga/wa* Sister *ni morau*	2	5
		others	2	1
2	Girl → Boy	**Girl** *ga/wa* Boy *ni ageru*	9	3
		Girl *ga/wa* **Boy** *ni kureru*	4	10
		Boy *ga/wa* Girl *ni morau*	2	4
		others	1	2
	Boy → Boy 2	**Boy** *ga/wa* Boy 2 *ni ageru/yaru*	11	13
		others	5	3

In cartoon #1, (a) a boy gives candy to his sister, (b) the mother gives a balloon to the sister, and (c) the sister gives the balloon to the boy. Examples of sentences produced by a L2 learner and a native speaker are given in (8) and (9), respectively.

(8) *Otoko no ko wa imōto ni kyandī o <u>ageta</u> ... okāsan wa imōto ni barun o <u>yatta</u> ... imōto wa otoko no ko ni barun o <u>watashita</u>.*
 "The boy gave the candy to his sister ... the mother gave a balloon to the sister ... the sister handed the balloon to the boy." (L2L-10)

(9) *Otoko no ko wa imōto ni sono ame o <u>ageta</u> ... imōto wa okāsan ni fūsen o <u>moratta</u> ga, ... sore o otoko no ko ni <u>kureta</u>.*
 "The boy gave the candy to his sister ... the sister got a balloon from their mother, but ... gave it to the boy." (NS-08)

In order to describe situation (a), almost all of the participants (13 out of 16 L2 learners and 15 out of 16 native speakers) used the giving verb *ageru*, choosing the boy as the grammatical subject and agent of the action: this indicates that they took a neutral or the boy's viewpoint. To describe situations (b) and (c), however, a majority of L2 learners chose donatory expressions based on a neutral or the mother's (nine out of 16) and the sister's (10 out of 16) viewpoints, while many of the native speakers chose expressions based on the sister's (13 out of 16) and the boy's (11 out of 16) viewpoints, respectively.[11] As seen in (8), some L2 learners used a variety of verbs such as *yaru* "give" and *watasu*

---

[11] Three native speakers chose mostly *ageru* to describe the giving activity regardless of the given characters.

"hand," possibly in an attempt to show the relationship between the given characters (senior position versus junior position) as well as to avoid repeating the verb *ageru* "give" in their sentences. All of these verbs, however, indicate that the viewpoint is based on the agents of those actions. Native speakers, on the other hand, chose to use more often the donatory verbs *kureru* "give" and *morau* "receive" to describe situations (b) and (c), as shown in (9). As a result, the viewpoint commonly taken by L2 learners shifted to become Boy → Mother → Sister, while most of the native speakers took the viewpoint of Boy → Sister → Boy. This means that L2 learners often used a donatory expression based on the character who initiated an action. Native speakers, on the other hand, chose an expression based on the main character and, after the viewpoint shifted to another character when the exchange of things took place between two characters other than the main character, the viewpoint shifted back to the main character.

In cartoon #2, (a) a girl gives an apple to a boy, and (b) the boy gives the apple to another boy. Most of the L2 learners and native speakers (11 and 13 out of 16, respectively) used *ageru/yaru* to describe situation (b), in which the statement is given from a neutral or the boy's viewpoint. Differences between the two groups were observed in describing situation (a). Examples of sentences produced by a L2 learner and a native speaker are shown in (10) and (11), respectively.

(10) *Onna no ko wa sono otoko no ko ni ringo o ageru. Otoko no ko wa totemo ureshii. Soshite, otoko no ko wa ringo o kamō to suru to …*
"The girl gives the apple to the boy. The boy is very happy. Then, when the boy is about to take a bite of the apple … " (L2L-07)

(11) *Otoko no ko ga mitsumete iru to, onna no ko wa motte ita ringo no hitotsu o otoko no ko ni kuremashita. Otoko no ko ga moratta ringo o tabeyō to shite iru to …*
"When the boy was staring (at her), the girl gave him one of the apples that she had. When the boy was about to eat the apple that he received … " (NS-14)

As a result, similar to the case with cartoon #1, the viewpoint commonly taken by L2 learners shifted to become Girl → Boy, while the native speakers' viewpoint[12] stayed as Boy → Boy in describing cartoon #2.

---

[12] Two native speakers, who used *ageru* to describe situation (b) in the main clause, also used *kureru* or *morau* to describe situation (a) within a relative clause (e.g., *onna no ko ga kureta ringo o sono otoko no ko ni ageta* "(he) gave the boy the apple that the girl had given (him)"; *ima moratta ringo o sono otoko no ko ni agemashita* "(he) gave the boy the apple that he got just now"), thus taking the boy's viewpoint.

Table 4 shows the results for the number of donatory expressions that were used to describe the stories in cartoons #3 and #4, in which an exchange of favourable actions takes place among the given characters.

Table 4. Donatory expressions used in narratives: Cartoons #3 and #4

#		Structure with V-*te ageru/yaru*, V-*te kureru*, or V-*te morau*	L2Ls (n=16)	NSs (n=16)
3	Girl → Old man	**Girl** *ga/wa* Old man *ni/o* V-*te ageru*	1	3
		Old man *ga/wa* Girl *ni/o* V-*te morau*	2	0
		others	13	13
	Boy → Old woman	**Boy** *ga/wa* Old woman *ni/o* V-*te ageru*	3	10
		others	13	6
	Old woman → Boy	**Old woman** *ga/wa* Boy *ni/o* V-*te ageru/yaru*	1	1
		Old woman *ga/wa* **Boy** *ni/o* V-*te kureru*	0	6
		Boy *ga/wa* Old woman *ni/o* V-*te morau*	0	3
		others	15	8
4	Boy → Girl	**Boy** *ga/wa* Girl *ni* V-*te ageru*	3	12
		Girl *ga/wa* Boy *ni* V-*te morau*	2	0
		others	11	6
	Girl → Boy	**Girl** *ga/wa* Boy *ni* V-*te ageru*	2	2
		Girl *ga/wa* **Boy** *ni* V-*te kureru*	2	8
		Boy *ga/wa* Girl *ni* V-*te morau*	3	8
		others	9	3

In cartoon #3, (a) a girl helps an old man cross the street, (b) a boy tries to do an old woman the same favour, and (c) the old woman helps the boy cross the street. In describing situation (a), two L2 learners used expressions of the old man receiving assistance from the girl that employed *morau*, as in (12).

(12) *Ojīsan ga onna no ko ni michi o wataru no o tetsudatte moratta.*
 "The old man had the girl help him cross the road." (L2L-09)

Another learner used expressions of the old man being helped by the girl using the passive form (e.g., *ojīsan wa onna no ko ni tasukerarete imasu* "the old man is being helped by the girl"). In both of those sentences, the statement is made from the old man's viewpoint. None of the native speakers employed these expressions. To describe situation (b), more native speakers used the auxiliary V-*te ageru* than did L2 learners (10 and three, respectively). As a result, in those sentences produced by the native speakers, the viewpoint is placed on the boy. In order to describe situation (c), most of the L2 learners (15 out of 16) used expressions that have the old woman as the subject and do not include a donatory auxiliary verb. Some native speakers, on the other hand, used the donatory auxiliary verb V-*te kureru* (six out of 16) or V-*te morau* (three out of 16) to describe the same situation. Examples of sentences written by two L2 learners and two native speakers are given in (13) and (14), respectively:

(13) a. *Obāsan wa sono otoko no ko ga michi o wataru koto o tetsudatta.*
"The old woman helped the boy in crossing the street." (L2L-15)
b. *Obāsan wa kare no te o totte ōdanhodō o watarimashita.*
"The old woman took his hand and crossed the road." (L2L-04)

(14) a. *Sono obāsan wa otoko no ko ga michi o wataru no o tetsudatte kureta.*
"The old woman helped the boy in crossing the street." (NS-05)
b. *... sono obāsan ni otoko no ko ga te o hiite moratte ōdanhodō o wataru koto ni naru.*
"... the boy ends up crossing the road having his hand held by the old woman." (NS-12)

In such sentences produced by L2 learners, the viewpoint is neutral or placed on the old woman. Those expressions made by the native speakers, however, indicate that the statements are made from the boy's viewpoint. A further investigation reveals that among the "other" structures, seven out of 16 native speakers used passive verb forms (e.g., *Gyaku ni otoko no ko ga obāsan ni tasukerareru koto ni natta* "On the contrary, the boy ended up being helped by the old woman"). This indicates that native speakers employed voice instead of donatory expressions to maintain the boy's viewpoint in describing the same situation.

In cartoon #4, (a) a boy helps a girl ride a bicycle, and (b) the girl helps the boy ride a bicycle. A similar tendency to the one in cartoon #3 was observed here. In describing situation (a), more native speakers used the auxiliary V-*te ageru* than did L2 learners (12 and three, respectively). (15) and (16) represent examples of sentences produced by a L2 learner and a native speaker, respectively.

(15) *Shōjo ga saka o noboru tame ni shōnen ga ushiro kara jitensha o oshite iru.*
"The boy is pushing the bicycle from behind so the girl can go up the slope." (L2L-12)

(16) *Otoko no ko wa, onna no ko ga jitensha de sakamichi o noboru no o oshi<u>te</u> <u>agete</u> imasu.*
"The boy is pushing the girl so she can go up the hill on a bicycle."
(NS-01)

In such sentences, L2 learners objectively described the situation using bare verbs, while native speakers made the statements from the boy's viewpoint by using the auxiliary V-*te ageru*. Similarly, in describing situation (b), L2 learners mainly used bare verbs, whereas native speakers used the V-*te kureru* and V-*te morau* structures with a variety of verbs (e.g., *oshite/nosete moraimashita* "(the boy) had the girl push/ride (the bicycle),*" oshi<u>te</u> <u>kureru</u> yō ni tanomimashita* "(the boy) asked (the girl) to push"), thus placing the viewpoint on the boy.

In order to determine the overall tendency of narrative viewpoints taken by the participants in their compositions, the total number of donatory expressions that involved the main character (the boy) and other characters was calculated. Table 5 shows the number of occurrences of donatory verbs found in the 64 compositions about cartoons #1 and #2, and Table 6 shows the number of donatory auxiliary verbs that appeared in another 64 compositions about cartoons #3 and #4. The number of verbs in the tables reflects that of the exchange of things and favours that involved the main character and one other character in each story. The number of occurrences that involved activity between two characters other than the main character (i.e., panel 3 of cartoon #1: Mother → Sister, and panel 1 of cartoon #3: Girl → Old man) was not included in the total. If the participants referred to the same donatory event more than once in their compositions, only one expression that indicated the viewpoint[13] was included in the number. The viewpoint was determined as either Main or Other, based on the accompanying donatory verb and the associated case marker used in each sentence or clause.

Table 5. Donatory verbs and viewpoints: Cartoons #1 and #2

Donatory verbs	Viewpoint by Character			
	L2Ls (n=16)		NSs (n=16)	
	Main	Other	Main	Other
(*wa/ga*) ... *ageru/yaru*	24	19	30	4
(*ni*) ... *kureru*	6	0	16	0
(*wa/ga*) ... *morau*	4	2	9	0
Total	34	21	55	4

---

[13] For example, if a participant used both *ageru* and *morau* to describe the same donatory event, only *morau*, which does not include a neutral viewpoint, was included in the number.

Table 6. Donatory auxiliary verbs and viewpoints: Cartoons #3 and #4

Donatory auxiliary verbs	Viewpoint by Character			
	L2Ls (n=16)		NSs (n=16)	
	Main	Other	Main	Other
(wa/ga) ... V-te ageru/yaru	6	3	22	3
(ni/o) ... V-te kureru (wa/ga)	2	0	14	0
... V-te morau	3	2	11	0
Total	11	5	47	3

In terms of frequency, all of the participants used donatory verbs in their compositions to describe the exchange of things between the main character and one other character, and the total number of occurrences was about the same between L2 learners and native speakers: 55 and 59, respectively. In comparison with the use of bare donatory verbs, the occurrence of auxiliary verbs in L2 narratives was small in number (in total, 16). Seven out of 16 L2 learners did not use any donatory auxiliary verbs, while all of the 16 native speakers employed them when describing the activity of exchanging favours in the stories. This result is consistent with that of Watanabe (2012b), who reported that L2 learners used far fewer donatory auxiliary verbs than bare donatory verbs.

Regarding viewpoint, if we focus on the data generated by the activities of giving and receiving things and favourable actions that involved the main character and one other character in the four stories, the findings of the study suggest that L2 learners used *ageru/yaru* and V-*te ageru/yaru* most frequently in comparison with other donatory and auxiliary verbs and, as a result, the viewpoint was often placed on other characters rather than on the main character: in the case of donatory verbs, 21 out of 55 instances (38%), and in the case of auxiliary verbs, five out of 16 instances (31%). Distribution of choice between Main and Other made by the L2 learners was significantly different from that of the native speakers, both in their use of donatory verbs ($\chi^2(1)$=16.40, p<.01) and donatory auxiliary verbs ($\chi^2(1)$=7.26, p<.01). Similar to the findings of Okugawa (2007) and Watanabe (2012b), the native speakers in the present study maintained the main character's viewpoint, but the L2 participants did not. These results are also similar to those of Nakahama and Kurihara (2007) that reported the viewpoint shift among L2 learners and native speakers' tendency to fix the viewpoint on a single character. As a result, L2 learners' narratives that describe the exchange of things and favourable actions were often found to be somewhat less coherent even when they did not contain any overt grammatical errors. An example of sentences produced by a L2 learner is presented in (17).

(17) *Sono otoko no ko wa obāsan o tetsudatte-agetai to omotta. Demo, obāsan wa sono otoko no ko ga michi o wataru no o tetsudatte-yatta.*
"That boy thought he wanted to help the old woman. However, the old woman helped the boy cross the street." (L2L-13)

The second sentence in (17), which employs V-*te yaru*, indicates that the senior–junior relationship of the given characters (i.e., Old woman and Boy) was taken into consideration. As a result, however, the statement is made from the old woman's viewpoint.

3.3.3. L2 learners' compositions in English

In order to determine how L2 learners' use of certain Japanese deictic expressions might be affected by their L1 system, English compositions were collected from the L2 participants. After an interval, L2 learners were instructed to write about the same cartoon strips in English.

First, the learners' use of English demonstratives "this" and "that," the counterparts of Japanese *kore/kono* and *sore/sono*, was examined. Two examples of demonstratives that appeared in L2 learners' English compositions are shown in (18) and (19), which described parts of cartoon #1 and cartoon #2, respectively.

(18) … The little sister was very happy. She also got a balloon from her mom. But she gave that to her older brother because she wanted to thank him for the treats. (L2L-11)

(19) … Then, an even smaller boy comes along, and looks like he wants that apple. … (L2L-07)

Only a small number of "that"s that refer to or modify a thing (four instances in the entire 16 sets of compositions) were used, and no use of the demonstrative "this" was found in the English compositions. Watanabe (2010), who compared the use of the English demonstratives "this" and "that" with that of Japanese *kore/kono* and *sore/sono* in L1 narratives, reported that English speakers produced far more instances of "this" than "that," and that the prenominal "this" mostly appeared as indefinite "this N" when introducing a new character or thing in the story (e.g., "It's a simple story. [A]lright, there's um *this* penguin family. …" (p. 174)). Watanabe's data were from oral storytelling, while the present study used written compositions — this may have affected the results of each study in the frequency of the demonstratives "this" and "that." In the present study, in order to determine how the main character is referred to as a topic in the learners' L1 writing, the reference words indicating the boy in the story were also examined. Parts of the compositions that explained cartoon #3 and cartoon #4 are shown in (20) and (21), respectively.

(20) A boy watches as a girl leads an elderly man across an intersection. Then, the boy starts looking around. He sees an elderly lady, and offers to help her cross the street. ...   (L2L-03)

(21) A boy is pushing a girl along as she rides her bike. He's pushing her up a gentle hill. Then, the boy asks for a turn on the bike. ...   (L2L-14)

Unlike in Japanese, omission of subjects is not possible in English sentences: the main character was commonly introduced as "a boy," and when he is mentioned for the second time and onward, it was either marked by the definite article as in "the boy" or replaced with the pronoun "he" across the four compositions. In sum, in L2 learners' English writing, an overall lack of demonstratives and the use of other reference devices such as articles and pronouns were observed.

In order to compare the viewpoint in learners' Japanese and English compositions, the subject of each sentence or clause that included a verb related to a donatory activity in their English writing was also examined. One of the learners' 16 sets of English compositions is shown in (22), and the noun phrases that indicate the agents of the donatory actions are underlined.

(22) a. A young boy goes home with a bag of candy and shares it with his little sister. The mother gives the little sister a balloon and she shares it with her brother.
  b. ... The girl gives the second apple to the boy. He is about to eat it when he sees a little boy looking at him. ... The boy gives the apple to the little boy.
  c. A boy sees a girl helping an old man cross the street. After looking both ways, the boy sees an old woman and offers to help her cross the street too. Instead, the old woman takes him across the street.
  d. A boy is pushing a girl on a bicycle to go over a hill. Once they reach the top of the hill, ... the girl pushes from the back to help him go faster. ...   (L2L-05)

The results show that in the case of 14 out of 16 learners, their choice of the grammatical subject of the sentence or clause that described each donatory activity (e.g., "The mother" in (22a)) was identical between their Japanese and English compositions, even though one was not exactly a translation of the other. Also, within the English compositions, 13 out of 16 learners were identical in terms of their choice of subjects in the sentences or clauses that described donatory activities. The subject of each sentence or clause involving a donatory activity that was commonly taken by those learners shifted to be Boy → Mother → Sister for cartoon #1, Girl → Boy for cartoon #2, Girl → Boy → Old woman for cartoon #3, and Boy → Girl for cartoon #4 in their writing, as shown in (18a), (18b), (18c), and (18d), respectively. These results suggest that in their compositions both in English and Japanese, L2 learners described each giving–receiving event based on the character who initiated an action, thus maintaining a neutral viewpoint.

3.4. Discussion
3.4.1. Deictic expressions and cross-linguistic considerations

Overall, the results of this study suggest that L2 learners used Japanese demonstratives and donatory verbs in limited and different ways in comparison with native speakers. In the study, L2 participants had knowledge of those linguistic forms and, although the total number was smaller than what native speakers used, most of the learners employed at least some of those devices when describing the given events in the story. The differences between the native speakers and L2 learners in their use of deictic expressions, therefore, may not be so much due to the learners' lack of grammatical knowledge. Rather, the way the learners used those expressions in their L2 writing was likely influenced by the way they treat viewpoint in their L1 writing, as seen in the way they used reference words and chose the subjects of sentences in their English compositions. The following discusses how L2 learners' production of the target forms might be influenced by their L1 system.

Regarding the demonstratives, in addition to the overall lack of the *so*-series, L2 learners' use of *sono* + noun was mainly limited to referring to the main character of the story, where overgeneralization of the topic marker *wa* was also observed. Japanese native speakers, on the other hand, used topic omission in referring to the already introduced main character and employed the *so*-series when referring to a subsequently introduced secondary character, thing, or event. Yanagimachi (2000), who investigated the choice of referential forms made by English-speaking learners of Japanese in their narrative data, reported that the learners used overt reference more frequently than Japanese native speakers did. Yanagimachi's results suggest that when they were asked to retell a story in third-person contexts, L1 English speakers had difficulty using zero anaphora and employed full noun phrases instead in their narratives in Japanese. Yanagimachi further suggested that although L2 learners can achieve native-like frequency in zero pronouns in their first- and second-person narratives where discourse topics are easily recognized from the immediate context, they tend to produce overt referential forms in third-person narratives where it is the speaker's responsibility to decide from which character's viewpoint the given story should be told. In the present study, L2 learners who overused full noun phrases also did not fix the viewpoint on a specific character, while native speakers maintained the main character's viewpoint by utilizing topic omission when writing about the given story. Also, as Watanabe (2010) indicated in his study on Japanese and English prenominal demonstratives, although *sono* is found to be the unmarked demonstrative in the Japanese data, English prenominal demonstratives do not share the same function. L2 learners in the present study, who may employ other devices such as articles and pronouns than demonstratives as anaphoric reference in marking the current topic in their L1 system, have likely produced full noun phrases, and some of the learners marked the boy with *sono* in referring to the already introduced main character in their compositions in Japanese where topic omission is more acceptable.

As for the donatory expressions, the results of this study suggested that native speakers of Japanese tend to adapt the narrator's viewpoint to that of the main character and maintain that viewpoint when they describe the exchange of things and favourable actions using the donatory verbs and auxiliary verbs. L2 learners in the study, however, often shifted the viewpoint from character to character since they chose the donatory expressions based on the characters that initiated an action. Also, in comparison with native speakers, L2 learners did not appear to make full use of auxiliary verbs when describing the activity of giving and receiving favours, as opposed to exchanging things, in a story. As a result, L2 learners' narratives were found to be less natural than those of native speakers. Although the Japanese donatory verbs *ageru* and *kureru* both represent an action of giving, they eventually make the narrator take specific viewpoints: neutral or the giver's for *ageru*, and the receiver's for *kureru*. The verb *kureru* is "strongly subjective" (Iwasaki, 1993, p. 7) and allows the narrator to "empathize" with the personal referent (Kuno, 1987, p. 206). In other words, *kureru* is used when the narrator takes a subjective stance in describing a giving–receiving event from the receiver's viewpoint. The English verb "give," on the other hand, does not have the function of specifying a viewpoint. Moreover, the giving–receiving of a favourable action tends to be described with an action verb that is accompanied by a donatory auxiliary verb to indicate the viewpoint in Japanese: without such a linguistic device that indicates the narrator's personal involvement, "statements carrying only neutral information convey an overwhelming tone of inappropriateness" (Maynard, 1997, p. 126). In English, however, the same given action is commonly described in a neutral statement with the action verb alone. It could be natural for L2 learners, then, to use the more neutral *ageru* in place of *kureru*, as well as bare action verbs without auxiliaries, in describing the exchange of things and favourable actions when those linguistic devices are not available in their L1. Thus, the findings of the present study suggest that due to the differences in narrative viewpoint and related linguistic structures between English and Japanese, L2 learners produced fewer donatory verb *kureru* and auxiliary donatory verbs that are both unique to Japanese and do not share the same domains in their L1.

3.4.2. Deictic expressions and pedagogical implications

Demonstratives and donatory verbs that were examined in the present study are commonly considered as basic grammatical features of Japanese. However, without understanding the anaphoric use of the demonstratives *sore* and *sono*, as well as the close relationship of donatory verbs and the notion of viewpoint, L2 learners' grammatical knowledge of the forms alone may not necessarily translate into native-like use of them. In order to help L2 learners acquire the nuanced use of these deictic expressions, certain strategies could also be accommodated during instruction.

In the present study, the anaphoric function of the *so*-series, that is, to refer "to something that is not known personally to … the hearer or has not been a shared experience between them" (Kuno, 1978a, p. 290), appears to be reflected in Japanese native speakers' compositions. Most of the L2 learners, however, did not utilize the function of *sore* and *sono* + noun when they described people, things, and events that were mentioned in the preceding sentences in which the anaphoric use of the *so*-series both as pronouns and prenominal demonstratives is expected. In the Japanese language classroom, demonstrative words are generally introduced and reinforced as a grammatical feature that refers to people and things in relation to the physical location of the speaker and hearer. Thus, L2 learners are commonly exposed to the non-anaphoric or situational use of demonstratives when they learn and practise the words. However, the anaphoric use of demonstratives, especially what Kinsui and Takubo (1990) called the neutral form of demonstratives, the *so*-series, would also need to be emphasized in the classroom. In order for L2 learners to be aware of this, they may need to be instructed to pay special attention to their anaphoric use of demonstrative words when they engage in describing people and events in a story that do not necessarily provide immediate contexts. L2 learners could also be reminded that the *so*-series can be used with a non-restrictive relative clause to refer to the content of the previous sentence in their narratives (e.g., <u>Sore o mita otoko no ko wa</u> … "A boy who saw that … ").

Regarding the donatory expressions, the results of the present study showed that some of the L2 learners used *yaru*/V-*te yaru* to describe a situation where the donatory activity takes place between the main character and a character in a senior position (i.e., Mother and Old woman), indicating that those learners were aware of the hierarchical relationship between the given characters. Similar to demonstratives, donatory verbs are typically introduced in the Japanese language classroom with the notion of a speaker–hearer or self–other dichotomy. It is equally important that the notion of viewpoint is emphasized when L2 learners start using donatory expressions in narratives. It would be beneficial for L2 learners to know that in Japanese discourse, the narrator tends to take and maintain a subjective stance, and that some linguistic devices such as donatory verbs function to indicate "who the narrator empathizes with" and "from whose perspective the incident is described" (Maynard, 1998, p. 79). Moreover, formulaic expressions such as V-*te kuremasen ka* "Wouldn't you please ...?" and V-*te moraitai* "I would like you to ..." are often introduced and practised as set phrases in the Japanese language classroom, but L2 learners would also need to keep in mind that the exchange of favourable actions tends to be described with expressions that are closely associated with narrative viewpoint. However, as shown in the results of Watanabe's (2012b) study, which reported the overuse of the passive form of verbs in place of V-*te morau* among those learners who received instruction on perspective expressions, instruction to keep the viewpoint by using donatory expressions and passive sentences alone may not be sufficient. L2 learners would also need to be reminded about what sort of actions tend to be described by donatory auxiliary verbs (e.g., *tetsudau* → *tetsudatte-ageru* "to assist," *tasukeru* → *tasukete-kureru* "to help").

A further analysis of data in the present study indicates that L2 learners at the advanced level used topic omission more frequently and a wider variety of donatory verbs including *morau* and *kureru* than those at the intermediate level did.[14] However, no major differences were observed between the two levels in their use of donatory auxiliary verbs that describe the exchange of favourable actions. The interview results of Nakahama and Kurihara (2007) that investigated the expressions of viewpoint in L1 and L2 Japanese narratives indicate that L2 learners are largely unaware of the differences between Japanese and their L1 in terms of viewpoint setting,[15] or do not know exactly how to deliver a viewpoint in Japanese discourse. It can be said that there are certain deictic expressions that L2 learners may not necessarily acquire even though their proficiency increases, and that such expressions should be taught in a way that promotes the learners' awareness of Japanese viewpoint.

4. Conclusion

One of the limitations of the present study is the limited number of types of Japanese deixis that were examined through their overall frequency of use and basic functions in the narratives. In future research, it will be important to expand the investigation to incorporate a wider variety of deictic expressions, including the motion verbs *iku* and *kuru* as well as the auxiliary verbs V-*te iku* and V-*te kuru*, which will offer more detailed analyses. L2 learners' use of

---

[14] It was not possible to conduct a statistical analysis to compare the results between the two levels of proficiency in this study due to the small sample size and an imbalance in the number of participants (11 intermediate and 5 advanced).

[15] Nakahama and Kurihara (2007) reported that most of the L2 learners "were not aware of how Japanese focus on characters and center the story around them, instead of focusing on recounting facts or describing what happened" (p. 186) in discourse.

various types of deixis could also be compared across different L1s and different levels of proficiency. In order to better understand the characteristics of L2 learners' use of deixis, it would be beneficial to employ additional data collection methods such as stimulated recall and think-aloud protocol in future research. On the pedagogical side, it is also important to explore the effect of instructional intervention on the learning of deixis in Japanese.

Overall, due to the lack of demonstrative words and the choice of donatory expressions, L2 learners' written narratives are often found to be difficult to follow. It would benefit learners to become aware of the anaphoric use of demonstratives and pay attention to viewpoint when choosing donatory verbs so that they will be able to effectively describe a story in Japanese. The findings of this study suggest that in addition to understanding grammatical rules, it is important for L2 learners to acquire the preferred cognitive stances of language (e.g., Ikegami, 2005) in context in order to achieve better command of its deictic expressions.

Acknowledgements

I would like to thank the editors and the anonymous reviewers for their valuable comments and suggestions for earlier versions of this paper. Any remaining deficiencies are my own.

References

Anderson, S. & Keenan, E. L. (1985). Deixis. In T. Shopen (Ed.), *Language typology and syntactic description, Vol. 3* (pp. 259–308). Cambridge: Cambridge University Press.

Fillmore, C. (1997). *Lectures on deixis*. Stanford, CA: CSLI Publications.

Ikegami, Y. (1989). Nihongo hyōgen ron [Theories of Japanese discourse]. In K. Inoue (Ed.), *Nihon bunpō shōjiten* [A dictionary of Japanese grammar] (pp. 213–266). Tokyo: Taishukan.

Ikegami, Y. (2005). Indices of a 'subjectivity-prominent' language: Between cognitive linguistics and linguistic typology. *Annual Review of Cognitive Linguistics, 3*, 132–164.

Iwasaki, S. (1993). *Subjectivity in grammar and discourse*. Amsterdam: John Benjamins.

Kinsui, S. & Takubo, Y. (1990). Danwa kanri riron kara mita nihongo no shijishi [A discourse management analysis of Japanese demonstratives]. *Ninchi Kagaku no Hatten* [Advances in Cognitive Science], *3*, 85–115.

Kuno, S. (1978a). *The structure of the Japanese language*. Cambridge, MA: MIT Press.

Kuno, S. (1978b). *Danwa no bunpō* [Grammar of discourse]. Tokyo: Taishukan.

Kuno, S. (1987). *Functional syntax: Anaphora, discourse and empathy*. Chicago: University of Chicago Press.

Masuda, M. (2001). Danwa tengaigata rentaisetsu [On the discourse function of a type of non-restrictive relative clause in Japanese]. *Nihongo Kyōiku* [Journal of Japanese Language Teaching], *109*, 50–59.

Maynard, S. (1997). *Japanese communication: Language and thought in context*. Honolulu: University of Hawaii Press.

Maynard, S. (1998). *Principles of Japanese discourse: A handbook*. Cambridge: Cambridge University Press.

Nakahama, Y. & Kurihara, Y. (2007). Viewpoint setting in L1 and L2 Japanese narratives. *Studies in Language Sciences, 6*, 179–194.

Okugawa, I. (2007). Katari no danwa ni okeru shiten to jitai haaku [Viewpoint and cognitive construal in Japanese narrative discourse]. *Tsukuba Ōyō Gengogaku Kenkyū* [Tsukuba Journal of Applied Linguistics], *14*, 31–43.

Shoho, I. (1981). Ko-so-a no taikei [The system of ko-so-a]. In *Nihongo no shijishi* [Demonstratives in Japanese] (pp. 51–122). Tokyo: National Language Institute.

Watanabe, F. (2010). Clausal self-repetition and pre-nominal demonstratives in Japanese and English animation narratives. In P. Szatrowski (Ed.), *Storytelling across Japanese conversational genre* (pp. 147–180). Amsterdam: John Benjamins.

Watanabe, F. (2012a, March). Bogowasha to gakushūsha ni yoru nihongo monogatari sakubun ni okeru rentaishi to shite no shijishi no shiyō [Analysis of topic transition and referring expressions in native and non-native Japanese written narratives]. Paper presented at the American Association of Teachers of Japanese Annual Spring Conference, Toronto, Canada.

Watanabe, F. (2012b). Nihongo no katari no bunshō ni okeru shiten no hyōgen to sono shidō ni tsuite [On the use of perspective expressions and the effect of teaching them on their use in Japanese]. *Yamagata Daigaku Daigakuin Shakai Bunka Shisutemu Kenkyūka Kiyō* [Bulletin of Graduate School of Social and Cultural Systems at Yamagata University], *9*, 51–58.

Yanagimachi, T. (2000). JFL learners' referential-form choice in first-through third-person narratives. *Japanese Language Education around the Globe*. 109–128.

Appendix

Cartoons used in the elicitation task[16]

#1   #2   #3   #4

---

[16] The four cartoons were drawn by the author. The story of cartoon #3 was borrowed from the cartoonist Mr. Masashi Ueda's work "Kobo-chan" with his permission.

日本語学習者の物語作文におけるダイクシス表現：指示詞と授受動詞の場合

矢吹ソウ典子（ヨーク大学）

要旨

本研究は、日本語学習者による物語作文に現れたダイクシス表現の使われ方を調査した。特に作文中での指示詞「これ・この」「それ・その」および授受動詞「あげる・くれる・もらう」とその補助動詞の二種類のダイクシスに焦点をしぼり、結果を日本語母語話者のものと比較した。この調査の目的は、複数の登場人物が現れるストーリーについて語った際に見られる学習者の日本語ダイクシスの不充分あるいは不適切な使用の原因を探るものである。結果として、(1) 学習者の指示詞の使用は主にストーリーの主人公を示す「その」名詞節に限られていたこと、(2) 学習者はストーリー中の行動主に基いて授受表現を選ぶ傾向にあり、それが談話中で視点の移動を引き起こしていることが分かった。日本語学習者は談話の中で、指示語の照応用法的な使い方や授受動詞を選ぶ際の視点の置き方に注意を向ける必要がある。

Verbal short-term memory's phonological features in first- to seventh-grade Japanese EFL students

Yasuyuki SAKUMA, Fukushima University

Abstract
 This study investigated the effects of English language activities for Japanese elementary school students on phonological features of spoken English in verbal short-term memory. First- to seventh-graders ($N = 265$) took the Children's Test of English Nonword Repetition. Four main findings with pedagogical implications are reported. First, no student could pronounce nonwords or consonant clusters accurately, because of negative L1 transfer. Second, significant differences emerged for all students, except second-graders, in language familiarity effects for exact repetition of high- and low-rated wordlikeness, which seemed related to syllable number. Third, all students faced difficulties in retaining and producing stimuli when phonological information exceeded four syllables; even seventh-graders required repeated training. The results indicate that lower-grade students should be exposed to English information that uses fewer than four syllables to prevent exhausting their limited verbal short-term memory.

1. Role of verbal short-term memory in EFL students

 Although foreign language activities are mandatory for fifth- and sixth-graders in Japanese elementary schools, under the Course of Study that commenced in 2011 (Ministry of Education, Culture, Sports, Science and Technology [MEXT], 2008), few studies have highlighted linguistic features of cognitive development that are influenced by foreign language activities. Japanese elementary school students are not required to master linguistic knowledge (e.g., syntactic and phonological structures or vocabulary) or develop accurate English language expressions, as are Japanese junior high school (JHS) students. However, although objectives differ between JHS and elementary students, both must listen to and repeat spoken English accurately. The main focus of foreign language activities in elementary school is that of processing micro-units of phonological English information consisting of relatively small constituent elements, such as phonemes, rhythms and accents of words and phrases, to familiarize students with spoken English. This is considered essential for the macro-unit processing of phonological English information comprising larger segments of English text with multiple words, such as when reading aloud, listening, and speaking, which is required later in English language education.
 From a memory-development perspective, phonological features that serve as linguistic cues at the JHS and elementary level can affect language pro-

cessing at the micro level, such as prosody, thereby affecting students' awareness of, and ability to produce, phonologically accurate English during lessons. When students are asked to repeat English, they need to hear and temporarily retain the necessary phonological information in verbal short-term memory (STM)[1] — the part of working memory (WM) (Baddeley, Allen, & Hitch, 2011) that is essential for acquiring English as a foreign language (EFL) and for mastering one's first language (L1). However, verbal STM capacity, which increases from ages 5 to 15 (Gathercole & Alloway, 2008), is limited, and even same-age learners have different verbal STM capacities. In previous investigations (Sakuma, 2011; Sakuma & Saito, 2012), this author examined most of this study's participants for verbal STM capacity, considering Japanese as L1 and English as FL, using digit span tests (DSTs). The results suggested that higher-grade students tended to demonstrate longer spans. Therefore, among first- to seventh-graders, it can be assumed that higher-grade students with much larger verbal STMs can process complex language information such as nonwords with a higher number of syllables, low wordlikeness, and complicated phonological features, more quickly.

Several tests can be used to measure verbal STM, including the DST, which measures immediate serial recall of simple and familiar digits, such as 0 to 9, and the Children's Test of Nonword Repetition (CNRep; Gathercole & Baddeley, 1996), which measures immediate recall of 40 spoken nonwords across four groups with two, three, four, and five syllables, respectively. Although both the DST and the CNRep[2] measure verbal STM, and a strong positive correlation exists between the two tests, the ability to learn English vocabulary has been shown to have a consistently stronger and more specific link with the CNRep than with the DST. This is because the DST requires temporary storage and recall of simpler and more familiar phonological

---

[1] Verbal STM is a system for the temporary storage of verbal information (e.g., Baddeley, Gathercole, & Papagno, 1998). The system is denoted as a phonological loop in the working memory model (Baddeley et al., 2011).

[2] The DST is a sensitive measurement of phonological STM, a function that is supported by phonological knowledge of the language (Thorn & Gathercole, 1999). This instrument measures the capacity of verbal STM to store phonological information. Each of the two versions (Japanese as L1 and English as FL) randomly presents a sample of highly familiar numbers from 0 to 9. Each number can appear in a given sequence only once, and each increasing digit number includes two sets. Participants are asked to repeat the sequence of digits immediately after presentation. In scoring English DST for L2 learners, only the temporary storage and recall of definite successive digits is required; the quality of pronouncing English digits is not part of the evaluation. On the other hand, although CNRep also measures verbal STM, it does not directly measure the capacity of verbal STM. Scoring in the CNRep requires the temporary storage and recall of much more exact unfamiliar phonological sequences per each nonword, that is, the quality of their pronunciation.

stimuli, such as the participants' existing vocabulary knowledge, whereas the CNRep requires the temporary storage and recall of unfamiliar and more complicated phonological sequences similar to those of native English speakers (Gathercole, Willis, Baddeley, & Emslie, 1994). In short, unlike the DST, the CNRep requires exact phonological awareness and production of various phonological sequences that are similar to English vocabulary as exactly as possible. Children with relatively extensive knowledge of English vocabulary are more accurate when repeating those nonwords because they are more likely to have access to representations in long-term memory (LTM)[3] of familiar words that closely match the nonwords (Gathercole & Adams, 1993). Moreover, while the developmental association between English nonword repetition ability and English word learning may be strongest for English learners during the early school years, not only in L1 but also in L2, its significance extends into adulthood (Gathercole, Willis, Baddeley, & Emslie, 1994).

Therefore, the CNRep is a more powerful predictor of vocabulary acquisition in verbal STM than is the DST. This paper discusses phonological outcomes of Japanese elementary students' participation in foreign language activities from the verbal STM perspective, and focuses on their becoming familiar with English sounds and rhythms.

2. Children's test of nonword repetition

Gathercole and Baddeley (1996) developed the CNRep for children with English as their L1 and validated it with 612 children aged four to eight years. It is therefore regarded as appropriate for measuring children's verbal STM. It also reveals the level of phonological awareness required for L1 vocabulary acquisition (Gathercole & Baddeley, 1989; Michas & Henry, 1994; Gathercole, Hitch, Service, & Martin, 1997; Avons, Wragg, Cupples, & Lovegrove, 1998) and EFL (Service, 1992; Service & Kohonen, 1995; Masoura & Gathercole, 1999, 2005). The link between phonological awareness and the CNRep lies in verbal STM.

Regarding the relation between verbal STM (nonword repetition) and vocabulary acquisition, Gathercole (2006) highlighted the superiority of the phonological storage hypothesis; learners with higher phonological awareness levels and better nonword repetition skills can retain phonological information in verbal STM more accurately. In turn, accurately representing phonological

---

[3] Long-term memory is information stored in the brain that is retrievable over a long period of time. It is a complex storage system, with several different types of storage distribution. The system is partitioned into episodic, visual and auditory or verbal memory in the WM model (Baddeley et al., 2011). In this study, the focus was mainly on verbal information in LTM, such as numbers in the DST and phonological word sequences (e.g., phoneme, rhythm, accent, consonant clusters etc.) in CNRep.

information in verbal STM enables information rehearsal and transfer to LTM, leading to effective learning of new vocabulary.

The key processes that contribute to the CNRep occur over four stages: auditory processing on hearing information, phonological analysis based on the listeners' phonological awareness of phonotactic frequency, phonological storage or retention of phonological representations, and speech motor planning to produce language (Gathercole, 2006). Wordlikeness and prosody have the greatest influence on information processing in the CNRep.

Wordlikeness is a language-familiarity effect, whereby immediate memory is accessed when linguistic items are familiar (da Costa Pinto, 1991; Gathercole, Willis, Emslie, & Baddeley, 1991; Chincotta & Hoosain, 1995; Chincotta & Underwood, 1996, 1997; Thorn & Gathercole, 1999, 2001; Thorn, Gathercole, & Frankish, 2002; Munson, Kurtz, & Windsor, 2005; Vitevitch & Luce, 2005; Yuzawa & Saito, 2006). Therefore, familiar lexical items are supported by vocabulary and phonological knowledge, both influencing the two CNRep stages of phonological analysis and speech motor planning (Thorn, Gathercole, & Frankish, 2005). During phonological analysis, familiar nonwords linked to existing vocabulary and phonological knowledge are processed much faster and represented more accurately. In contrast, unfamiliar lexical items, including foreign words, are difficult to recognize, remember, and reproduce. Furthermore, during speech motor planning, if the phonological representation of nonwords degrades during retrieval of highly familiar nonwords, primed lexical representations can reintegrate them to fill in missing information by compensating with information from LTM. However, for less familiar nonwords, including foreign words, compensating for missing information by drawing on LTM is difficult.

Prosody refers to stress, pitch, pauses, speed, rhythm, intonation patterns, and other nonword features required for accurate verbal production. These can influence the CNRep scores (Roy & Chiat, 2004; Yuzawa, Miki & Saito, 2006; Chiat & Roy, 2007; Yuzawa, Masamichi, Yuzawa, Miki, Sekiguchi, & Li, 2012; Yamaguchi, Shimizu, Hijikata, & Imai, 2013).

Previous studies have examined non-Japanese (Finnish) primary school EFL students, finding positive correlations, not only between English pseudo-word repetition (verbal STM) and English reading, listening, and writing (Service, 1992) but also between pseudo-word repetition and English vocabulary learning (Service & Kohonen, 1995). In addition, Masoura and Gathercole (1999, 2005) reported a positive correlation between English nonword repetition and English vocabulary acquisition in primary school students, finding that students performed better on the CNRep in L1 than in English.

However, previous studies with Japanese EFL learners found no significant positive correlations between CNRep scores and a Teaching of English for International Communication-Institutional Program (TOEIC-IP) test for Japanese seventh-graders exposed to an English immersion program for approximately seven years (Yamaguchi, Shimizu, Hijikata, & Imai, 2013). Moreover, international kindergarten children with greater exposure to English prior to elementary school received lower EFL CNRep scores for five-syllable nonwords than did same-age native English speakers (Yuzawa et al., 2012). This was attributed to a lack of EFL phonological knowledge and constraints on EFL nonword repetition imposed by L1 phonological knowledge, as well as a negative transfer of prosodic features such as rhythm (Japanese mora-timed rhythm vs. English stress-timed rhythm), accent (Japanese pitch accent vs. English stress accent), and phonotactics (e.g., consonant clusters).

Differences demonstrated by Japanese and non-Japanese participants in the nonword repetition test make examination of the differences between L1 and English vocabularies necessary. The three main causal factors are accent, English learning goals, and the written communication system. Finnish and Greek students have strong and weak accents similar to those of English, whereas Japanese students have a pitch accent. Furthermore, Finnish students learn spoken and written English through listening, speaking, reading, and writing, beginning in the third grade. Because their L1 is alphabetic, they recognize written English information more easily than do Japanese students. Greek is the oldest surviving language in the Indo-European language family; more than 10 percent of English words are borrowed from Greek. Therefore, Greek native speakers may be familiar with some English vocabulary. The different correlations between CNRep scores and English linguistic knowledge for these EFL learners suggest that phonological knowledge of wordlikeness and prosody in LTM for words similar to English may enable phonological representation retention during phonological storage, and output during speech motor planning.

Three main points distinguish previous studies from this research: teaching content, evaluation, and participants. First, previous studies on English nonword repetition in L1 and EFL focused on learners acquiring a better knowledge of written and spoken English. However, no comparable research has been undertaken for elementary school learners seeking only to become familiar with English sounds and rhythms, and who's educational experience is based solely on the Japanese MEXT curriculum rather than formal lessons (e.g., private English-language schools).

Second, in previous studies CNRep evaluations have focused only on whether learners repeated nonwords accurately. The CNRep exact repetition scores for Japanese students in international kindergartens and immersion schools with high English language exposure were unexpectedly low. This study's participants attended a public elementary school with low English exposure; therefore, high attainment of exact CNRep repetition scores was unlikely. Prosodic differences make it difficult even for Japanese EFL learners with adequate English language exposure to repeat English nonwords exactly. In this study, investigating phonological features of spoken English in verbal STM required analysis of exact nonword repetition and prosodic features such as number of syllables, rhythm, accent[4], and consonant clusters as phonological sub-classifications. Thus, the evaluation had four categories: evaluation 1 (exact repetition), evaluation 2 (correspondence with the number of syllables), evaluation 3 (appropriate rhythm and accent), and evaluation 4 (clear consonant cluster). The prosodic features of EFL Japanese learners were examined. To repeat English nonwords with appropriate rhythm and accent, the participants had to produce phonological information for about a second, with clear strong and weak accent forms and appropriate stress-timed rhythm. If they could not produce nonwords quickly, their pronunciation could not be judged accurately for the appropriate rhythm and accent. In contrast, if they could not produce nonwords quickly, but they produced the correct number of syllables, their pronunciation was judged as corresponding to the correct number of syllables only if the fixed number of syllables was apparent with a slightly longer processing time. Japanese has mora-timed rhythm; therefore, Japanese EFL learners tend to recognize syllables in nonwords and reproduce nonwords with the correct number of syllables more easily than reproducing the appropriate rhythm and accent.

Third, Gathercole and Baddeley's original study (1996) in L1 focused on four- and six-year-old children; previous EFL studies focused mainly on specific elementary school grades (Service, 1992; Service & Kohonen, 1995; Masoura & Gathercole, 1999, 2005). In contrast, the present study focused on a cross-section of students from the first to seventh grades, not only at different stages of cognitive development and with different verbal STM capacities (Sakuma, 2011)[5] but also with different amounts of total English exposure[6]. Therefore, we expected that higher-grade students, who had not only larger

---

[4] Accent was judged mainly from the balance of strong and weak stress; it was not judged on the subtle distinction between the first accent and the second accent.
[5] In an investigation of Japanese and English DSTs conducted with almost the same sample as the one used in the present study, Sakuma (2011) reported that students in higher school grades tended to have greater STM capacities in the two languages.
[6] This study analyzed the data of the third year of the project. The third- to sixth-graders took English lessons as activities at elementary school for three years, while the seventh-graders took English lessons as activities at elementary school for two years and as a subject at junior high school. The first-graders took English activities for only a year and the second-graders took English activities for two years. The different English lesson periods and the school grades show the different total English exposure — the higher school grades become, the more English exposure increases. The relationship between English exposure and school grades is shown in detail in Section 3.2 of this paper.

verbal STM capacities but also much greater total knowledge of English phonological sequences, due to the effects of increased total English exposure, would achieve higher scores in producing words with a higher cognitive burden, such as nonwords and words with more syllables and low wordlikeness[7]. Specifically, for wordlikeness, if the students showed abundant vocabulary knowledge and elaborate phonological knowledge of spoken English, they were expected to produce nonwords with high wordlikeness more accurately through phonological analysis and speech motor planning — two key processes measured by the CNRep.

No previous study has examined a wide range of students attending English classes, framed through activities or focused on prosodic features in CNRep processing. Therefore, to examine verbal STM, this study collected basic data from a cross-section of students participating only in English communicative task-based activities, rather than formal form-based instruction.

This study focused on the following research questions (RQs):

RQ1: Does school grade influence accurate EFL nonword repetition in terms of the number of syllables?

RQ2: Does school grade influence prosodic abilities, including number of syllables, rhythm, accent, and consonant clusters, in EFL nonwords in terms of the number of syllables?

3. Method
3.1. English language exposure

To investigate the effects of English language activities including songs and games to familiarize students with spoken English, we selected students with poor EFL exposure prior to attending school English language activities. We focused on these students because attendance at English conversation schools and/or private lessons outside elementary school (as is often available in urban areas) would unavoidably affect student exposure to spoken and written English and other linguistic knowledge (e.g., grammar). The majority of students in this study had no previous exposure to English in school and no experience of studying abroad. Few students with limited EFL exposure prior to participating in English language activities at school were included in the

---

[7] Performance on the CNRep test can be influenced by the cognitive development and greater L1 abilities that accompany the increase in participants' age. However, for native English speakers, Gathercole et al. (1994) reported that nonword repetition ability may develop very slowly beyond eight years of age. Therefore, the age of participants in the present study may not have had a strong, direct effect on their performance. In addition, the research design makes it difficult to demonstrate a connection between L1 abilities and performance. These influences need further consideration as research problems.

present study.

This study took place in the third year of the Elementary School English-Language Activities Promotion Project at a rural site, before foreign language activities became mandatory in 2011. However, the school's goals and curriculum were almost identical to those recommended by MEXT for foreign language activities. Therefore, this study uses the terms 'English language activities' and 'foreign language activities' synonymously.

During this project's three-year span, the chief curriculum coordinator for English language activities, who also taught English language activities, prepared and administered the curriculum after coordinating with other teachers regarding content and teaching materials. The project's content focused on spoken English, listening and speaking, through games, songs, cards, chants, picture books, and worksheets. Written English was indirectly communicated through cards, worksheets, and picture books, but reading and writing were not taught systematically. In addition to organizing English activity classes, all teachers attempted to create an environment that provided opportunities for daily exposure to English, in both the school and the classroom, by organizing assemblies involving the entire student body and posting pictures, letters of the alphabet, and simple English words related to monthly units as notices on bulletin boards and along corridors. Following standard formal procedures, prior to the study, researchers obtained informed consent on the detailed research content (research purpose, expected duration, procedures, etc.) from the participants' parents through documents distributed by the town's superintendent of education and the school principal.

English classes were conducted during regular school terms. To enable students' involvement in communicative tasks, team teaching was employed with the homeroom teacher and an assistant language teacher (ALT) from the United States. The ALT was employed by the town's board of education (one ALT, a woman, taught all classes in the project's first year; another ALT, a man, taught in the second and third years).

3.2. Participants

Participants in the first and second grades took 20 English language activity classes annually (45 mins per class); participants in the third to sixth grades took 35 classes annually. The numbers of participants in each grade and the total numbers of English language activity classes per age group were as follows: 34 first-graders participated in 20 classes; 27 second-graders in 40 classes; 45 third-graders in 75 classes; 54 fourth-graders in 90 classes; 44 fifth-graders in 105 classes; and 43 sixth-graders in 105 classes. Furthermore, as a follow-up survey, tests were administered to 18 seventh-graders who had participated in the same project during the previous two years, for a total of 175 classes: 35 classes (45 mins per class) for each of the fifth and sixth grades, and 105 classes (50 mins per class) for the seventh grade (the first grade of junior high school). The total number of English lessons per grade included all classes conducted over the academic year, but excluded classes in which tests were administered. Therefore, the total number of classes (exposures) increased for higher grades, with only fifth- and sixth-graders having the same numbers of classes.

3.3. Materials and procedure

During August and September of the project's third year, the CNRep was administered individually in a quiet room, along with other tests not discussed here. Individual tests took approximately 20 mins, although the time required differed according to student responses. Before this study, the original 40 CNRep nonword test had been conducted with other cognitive tests on other elementary school children as a pilot study; the results indicated that the children found the tests a considerable burden, with many students, especially those in younger age groups, unable to focus sufficiently when asked to repeat some of the 40 nonwords. Therefore, we assumed that using 40 CNRep nonwords would probably impose a heavy cognitive burden, thus reducing the students' ability to focus and use their STM resources and preventing accurate determination of CNRep scores. Hence, we reduced the number of nonwords from the original 40 to 26.

Each nonword either strongly (high wordlikeness) or barely (low wordlikeness) resembled an actual word. Wordlikeness ratings were taken from Gathercole et al. (1991), a study in which 20 native English-speaking adults judged each spoken nonword on a five-point scale ranging from one (highly unlike a real word) to five (highly like a real word). Of six nonwords with two syllables, three were high (e.g., *pennel*) and three low (e.g., *tafflest*) in wordlikeness; of seven nonwords with three syllables, four were high (e.g., *commerine*) and three low (e.g., *frescovent*) in wordlikeness; of seven nonwords with four syllables, three were high (e.g., *commeecitate*) and four low (e.g., *woogalamic*); and of six nonwords with five syllables, three were high (e.g., *voltularity*) and three low (e.g., *detratapillic*).

The tests were administered according to the standard procedure for the CNRep. Briefly, each child was required to listen to a sequence played from a mini-disc (MD) on an MD recorder (RX-MDX81-S, Panasonic; Tokyo, Japan) and to pronounce the nonwords immediately after listening to each stimulus. The pronunciations were recorded on an IC recorder (HM-200, Sanyo; Tokyo, Japan), and the data (i.e., their pronunciations) were collected for subsequent analysis. Both the nonword stimuli and the instructions were recorded on the MD, which every student used to participate. The nonword items[8] were

---

[8] During the recording of CNRep nonwords, the English-speaking university instructor

pronounced by an English-speaking university teacher from the United Kingdom, who had been teaching English to Japanese university students for more than 30 years, and the present study's author recorded other instructions in Japanese. Each item in this session was presented at a rate of one nonword per second. Before the actual test administration, participants completed a practice version of one nonword to ensure that they understood how to respond. During the actual test, the participants repeated each item into the IC recorder microphone immediately after listening to the item. If they were unable to pronounce the item correctly and fluently, the experimenter encouraged them to pronounce as much as possible.

3.4. Scoring and analysis

As in Gathercole and Baddeley (1996), each CNRep stimulus was scored 0 (zero) or 1, with '1' indicating acceptable performance and '0' unacceptable performance. Gathercole and Baddeley (1996) found that mean L1 scores (the proportion of exact repetitions for all nonwords) for four-year-olds on items with two to five syllables were 7.0 (.7), 5.0 (.5), 3.0 (.3), and 4.0 (.4), respectively, from a possible 10.0 points, with a mean total score of 19 (.48). For six-year-olds, respective scores were 8.0 (.8), 6.0 (.6), 5.0 (.5), and 6.0 (.6), with a mean total score of 25 (.63).

Gathercole and Baddeley (1996) stated that nonword reproduction could easily be judged as correct or incorrect in most cases. However, testers had to score some cases as correct, even though some responses were not perfect, based on a rule of thumb: whether a listener who knew the child being tested, but who had not heard the taped items, could correctly reproduce the original nonword from the child's repetition. When children produced ambiguous or other similar-sounding responses, the rule of thumb was employed. A straightforward case would be that of a child with a strong regional accent for whom consistent deviations from received pronunciation would be expected in spontaneous speech as a direct consequence of the child's immature speech production skills rather than STM problems; these deviations were typically, highly systematic errors and phoneme substitutions. Another straightforward case would be that of a child who consistently replaced the sound 'c' with the sound 't' in spontaneous speech, such as saying *tontraponist* for *contraponist* in the CNRep. Moreover, in previous studies evaluating EFL Japanese learners, researchers familiar with phonological features of Japanese English scored 1 as

---

from the United Kingdom pronounced nonwords according to the International Phonetic Alphabet (IPA), as shown in Gathercole et al. (1994). It is assumed that pronunciation differences between a UK native speaker administering this CNRep and a US native speaker conducting English language activities would not directly affect nonword repetition ability.

correct for responses judged approximate to original nonwords. Therefore, EFL Japanese responses in evaluation 1 were scored 1 if the reproduction was not perfectly consistent with, but largely close to, the original nonwords. Japanese EFL learners face particular difficulties reproducing consonant clusters in evaluation 4, as reported by Li, Yuzawa, & Sekiguchi (2009). Therefore, in this study, some cases in evaluation 1 were scored 1 even if the scoring for evaluation 4 was incorrect. In contrast, because evaluations 2, 3, and 4 focused on specific phonological subcategories, some cases were scored 0 in evaluation 1 even if some scores from evaluations 2, 3, and 4 were scored 1 (correct). Overall, however, if a score of 1 was given in evaluation 1, a score of 1 was also given for evaluations 2 and 3 (except for consonant clusters in evaluation 4). However, in evaluation 3, for some accents, a combination of rhythm and accent for multisyllabic (two- to five-syllable) nonwords could ensure a regular, simple rhythm. Therefore, this combination was considered a useful, simple method for judging nonword repetition intuitively and immediately.

To ensure fair judgment of each student's responses, three native English speakers, accustomed to teaching English to Japanese students, analyzed spoken data on the IC recorder. The CNRep's inter-rater reliability was calculated; all three judges evaluated scores, and their majority opinion was considered the final judgment. Therefore, inter-rater reliability was $\alpha = .67$. Based on previous studies, this coefficient can be considered reliable as $r = .77$ (a test-retest reliability coefficient), 66 (a split-half reliability coefficient) (Gathercole & Baddeley, 1996), and $k = .713$ (Yamaguchi et al., 2013).

A two-way analysis of variance (ANOVA) was used with the variables grade level and number of syllables for the CNRep scores in RQs 1 and 2. A t-test for high and low wordlikeness was employed to examine the influence of the CNRep's two stages: phonological analysis and speech motor planning.

4. Results and discussion

4.1. Descriptive statistics

Before examining the two RQs, we analyzed the average proportions for wordlikeness from all grades to evaluate the language familiarity effect of English vocabulary and phonological knowledge. Table 1 shows descriptive statistics regarding evaluation 1 (exact repetition), evaluation 2 (correspondence with the number of syllables), evaluation 3 (appropriate rhythm and accent), and evaluation 4 (clear consonant clusters).

For evaluation 1, exact repetition, Gathercole and Baddeley (1996) reported that, for four-year-olds, the mean total score, without discriminating between high and low wordlikeness, was .48. In this study, only the mean score for high wordlikeness in the seventh grade (.52) exceeded this value (.48), as shown in Table 1. Compared to the average proportion of L1 children, this low score indicates limited vocabulary knowledge and some phonological knowledge, but an inferior EFL language familiarity effect for rudimentary phonological analysis and speech motor planning. However, this study's comparison of the average proportion of Japanese EFL learners, from first to seventh grade, indicates that scores for both high and low wordlikeness tended to be higher for higher-grade students (except sixth-graders) than for lower-grade students. This indicates an effect of increased language familiarity, owing to further cognitive development and higher exposure to English. For evaluations 2 and 3, wordlikeness across different grades showed a tendency similar to that in evaluation 1.

Table 1. CNRep descriptive statistics for wordlikeness for evaluations 1 to 4

	Evaluation 1				Evaluation 2				Evaluation 3				Evaluation 4			
	Wordlikeness				Wordlikeness				Wordlikeness				Wordlikeness			
	High		Low		High		Low		High		Low		High		Low	
Grade	M	SD	M	SD	M	SD	M	SD	M	SD	M	SD	M	SD	M	SD
1	0.20	0.19	0.12	0.19	0.54	0.24	0.45	0.21	0.44	0.23	0.40	0.25	0.06	0.12	0.04	0.07
2	0.22	0.14	0.18	0.17	0.65	0.26	0.53	0.20	0.53	0.24	0.54	0.23	0.03	0.05	0.03	0.05
3	0.32	0.16	0.23	0.16	0.74	0.16	0.58	0.15	0.65	0.16	0.62	0.19	0.05	0.07	0.06	0.08
4	0.38	0.16	0.25	0.15	0.71	0.16	0.58	0.16	0.61	0.20	0.58	0.20	0.04	0.08	0.03	0.04
5	0.40	0.15	0.29	0.15	0.74	0.16	0.62	0.14	0.63	0.17	0.66	0.17	0.05	0.07	0.07	0.09
6	0.28	0.15	0.18	0.13	0.69	0.18	0.56	0.17	0.52	0.23	0.49	0.22	0.06	0.15	0.05	0.11
7	0.52	0.17	0.34	0.18	0.77	0.15	0.65	0.11	0.68	0.14	0.75	0.16	0.11	0.13	0.14	0.16

In contrast, evaluation 4 revealed a floor effect for wordlikeness, indicating that the statistical analyses (t-tests) were insignificant. Therefore, we removed evaluation 4 data from this wordlikeness analysis and analyzed the significant association between student performances with high and low wordlikeness for evaluations 1 to 3, as shown in the later "Wordlikeness" section.

Table 2 shows descriptive statistics for the CNRep in the seven grades for the four evaluations. Each evaluation's overall features were as follows. For evaluation 1, score proportions for the total and for each syllable tended to be higher in the higher grades (except the sixth) than in the lower grades. Moreover, this evaluation (exact repetition) has been used to assess phonological features of verbal STM in prior studies of both L1 speakers and Japanese EFL learners. To investigate significant effects of teaching English in Japanese elementary schools through activities that focus mainly on familiarizing students with spoken English, we analyzed phonological reproduction of verbal STM by comparing similar CNRep scores for L1 children and EFL Japanese learners from prior studies. Seventh-graders attained the highest total CNRep score of .44, lower than the score for four-year-old native English speakers (.48) in Gathercole and Baddeley (1996). The study by Yamaguchi et al. (2013) on Japanese EFL seventh-graders in an immersion school produced a score of .55. In this study, therefore, the effect of English activities on phonological production was lower.

Table 2. CNRep descriptive statistics for evaluations 1 to 4

Syllable	Grade	Evaluation 1		Evaluation 2		Evaluation 3		Evaluation 4	
		M	SD	M	SD	M	SD	M	SD
2	1	0.17	0.19	0.79	0.27	0.65	0.30	0.05	0.11
	2	0.23	0.17	0.82	0.26	0.73	0.31	0.06	0.14
	3	0.26	0.19	0.89	0.13	0.86	0.15	0.05	0.10
	4	0.29	0.18	0.87	0.18	0.79	0.27	0.05	0.14
	5	0.37	0.21	0.90	0.16	0.83	0.22	0.02	0.07
	6	0.26	0.16	0.90	0.16	0.74	0.32	0.03	0.07
	7	0.37	0.16	0.86	0.18	0.82	0.21	0.03	0.06
3	1	0.21	0.26	0.61	0.30	0.50	0.31	0.04	0.10
	2	0.21	0.19	0.69	0.29	0.51	0.27	0.02	0.07
	3	0.35	0.21	0.83	0.18	0.74	0.23	0.11	0.14
	4	0.36	0.23	0.81	0.21	0.70	0.26	0.05	0.11
	5	0.36	0.23	0.81	0.21	0.66	0.24	0.05	0.12
	6	0.31	0.25	0.75	0.23	0.55	0.30	0.03	0.08
	7	0.53	0.28	0.90	0.15	0.77	0.17	0.03	0.10
4	1	0.15	0.23	0.43	0.24	0.31	0.30	0.02	0.07
	2	0.24	0.17	0.64	0.19	0.51	0.28	0.06	0.11
	3	0.31	0.21	0.67	0.16	0.55	0.22	0.06	0.11
	4	0.33	0.20	0.70	0.15	0.52	0.26	0.05	0.09
	5	0.42	0.20	0.77	0.17	0.66	0.27	0.05	0.12
	6	0.23	0.16	0.67	0.22	0.46	0.30	0.09	0.13
	7	0.48	0.21	0.83	0.13	0.71	0.16	0.07	0.17
5	1	0.12	0.21	0.31	0.32	0.22	0.29	0.06	0.17
	2	0.13	0.18	0.48	0.31	0.39	0.25	0.04	0.13
	3	0.20	0.24	0.55	0.27	0.44	0.28	0.05	0.15
	4	0.28	0.21	0.48	0.28	0.36	0.30	0.07	0.12
	5	0.26	0.21	0.56	0.26	0.41	0.25	0.19	0.24
	6	0.15	0.17	0.47	0.27	0.29	0.26	0.12	0.20
	7	0.35	0.29	0.69	0.25	0.55	0.30	0.12	0.17
Total	1	0.16	0.19	0.54	0.25	0.42	0.24	0.05	0.09
	2	0.20	0.13	0.66	0.25	0.54	0.24	0.03	0.04
	3	0.28	0.15	0.74	0.16	0.65	0.18	0.06	0.06
	4	0.32	0.14	0.72	0.17	0.59	0.21	0.03	0.05
	5	0.35	0.13	0.76	0.17	0.64	0.18	0.06	0.07
	6	0.24	0.13	0.70	0.20	0.51	0.23	0.05	0.12
	7	0.44	0.17	0.82	0.14	0.71	0.14	0.13	0.14

Note. Scores are shown as proportions. Evaluation 1, exact repetition; Evaluation 2, correspondence with the number of syllables; Evaluation 3, appropriate rhythm and accent; Evaluation 4, clear consonant clusters.

For total prosodic features (evaluations 2, 3, and 4), all scores in evaluation 2 and most scores in evaluation 3 (except first year) were greater than half (.50), with seventh-graders showing the highest score proportions in both evaluations. In contrast, scores for evaluation 4 (clear consonant clusters) were considerably lower across all grades. Most scores for the number of syllables across grades were <.01, indicating a floor effect as participants were influenced by negative L1 transfer across both age-range and cognitive-development levels. Japanese EFL learners, familiar with mora-timed rhythm since infancy (Li et al., 2009), have difficulty in hearing consonant clusters in English nonwords, such as *perplisteronk* and *versatrationist* because these are not part of the Japanese syllabary. The low scores in these categories suggest that elementary and early junior high school students may not yet have exact auditory processing phonological awareness; therefore, they may be unable to achieve exact production during speech motor planning.

4.2. Exact repetition (Evaluation 1)

For evaluation 1 (exact repetition), a two-way ANOVA was conducted, in which the dependent variables were the CNRep scores for evaluation 1 (Table 2). ANOVA results did not indicate significant interaction between grade level and number of syllables ($p = .173$); only main effects were significant [grade: $F(6, 257) = 11.06$, $p < .001$, $\eta^2 = .11$; number of syllables: $F(2.88, 740.66) = 20.54$, $p < .001$, $\eta^2 = .03$]. Therefore, for RQ1, grade-level influence on accurate nonword repetition in EFL was not differentiated by the number of syllables, and differences in evaluation 1 were attributed only to grade level and number of syllables. Grade-level influence on evaluation 1 was identical for every syllable level, with higher grades showing better exact repetition, regardless of the number of syllables. Therefore, only grade level indicated differences not only in verbal STM capacities but also in total English exposure by age. An increased number of syllables may be burdensome to lower-grade students because processing such phonological information may exceed their STM capacity. Higher-grade students can process many syllables more easily, because they are more likely to have larger verbal STM capacities. Furthermore, as higher-grade students have a greater exposure to English, their LTM has been more involved in English language processing, and because they have higher cognitive abilities they can produce phonological nonwords immediately without using too much verbal STM capacity.

4.3. Prosodic features (Evaluations 2, 3, and 4)

For evaluation 2 (correspondence with the number of syllables) a two-way ANOVA was conducted for all grades. The dependent variables were CNRep scores from evaluation 2 (Table 3) and the independent variables were grade and number of syllables. ANOVA results showed significant main effects for grade and number of syllables [grade: $F(6, 258) = 8.20$, $p < .001$, $\eta^2 = .08$; number of syllables: $F(2.68, 692.56) = 192.09$, $p < .001$, $\eta^2 = .22$] and significant interaction between grade and number of syllables [$F(16.11, 692.56) = 2.78$, $p < .001$, $\eta^2 = .02$].

Table 3. Two-way ANOVA of effects of school grade level and number of syllables (Evaluation 2)

Source	df	SS	MS	F	p		η^2
Between Subjects							
Grades	6	5.77	0.96	8.20	< .001	***	.08
Error	258	30.28	0.12				
Within Subjects							
The number of syllables	2.68	16.42	6.12	192.09	< .001	***	.22
The number of syllables x Grades	16.11	1.43	0.09	2.78	< .001	***	.02
Error (The number of syllables)	692.56	22.05	0.03				
Total	975.35	75.94					

Note. ***$p < .001$. η^2 = Effect size.

As a post hoc analysis, a Bonferroni adjustment was conducted. The results (Table 4) show some differences across the number of syllables, such as two vs. three; three vs. four, and many syllable combinations were significant. Scores for low numbers of syllables were significantly higher than those for high numbers of syllables. No significant differences were observed in comparisons across numbers of syllables in seventh-grade students, except between four and five syllables. This robustness in up to four syllables may indicate that abilities subject to cognitive development, such as STM capacity and the ability to recognize the number of syllables, may be involved in relatively small informational units. In comparison with the no-interaction result in evaluation 1, overall, four- and five-syllable comparisons across all grades revealed significant differences, possibly attributable to differences in cognitive burden. In contrast to the macro-level task of evaluation 1, evaluation 2 was a micro-level task, involving correspondence with the number of syllables, and thus possibly considered easier because participants were required to pronounce only a fixed number of syllables very slowly, without rhythm; therefore, the cognitive burden was lower although the number of syllables was slightly higher.

Table 4. Post hoc analysis Bonferroni adjustment for evaluation 2

		2 vs. 3		2 vs. 4		2 vs. 5		3 vs. 4		3 vs. 5		4 vs. 5	
Evaluation	Grade	p	d	p	d	p	d	p	d	p	d	p	d
	1	<.001 ***	0.65	<.001 ***	1.42	<.001 ***	1.64	<.001 ***	0.65	<.001 ***	0.96	.007 **	0.43
	2	.001 ***	0.48	<.001 ***	0.80	<.001 ***	1.19	.269	0.20	.001 ***	0.69	.002 **	0.63
	3	.025 **	0.42	<.001 ***	1.51	<.001 ***	1.58	<.001 ***	0.90	<.001 ***	1.17	.003 **	0.52
2	4	.056	0.27	<.001 ***	1.00	<.001 ***	1.64	<.001 ***	0.62	<.001 ***	1.36	<.001 ***	1.00
	5	.002 **	0.51	<.001 ***	0.77	<.001 ***	1.59	.362	0.16	<.001 ***	1.04	<.001 ***	0.99
	6	<.001 ***	0.73	<.001 ***	1.16	<.001 ***	1.93	.020 **	0.35	<.001 ***	1.12	<.001 ***	0.81
	7	.452	0.22	.572	0.17	.007 **	0.79	.230	0.45	.001 ***	1.02	.017 *	0.73

Note. $*p < .05$. $**p < .01$. $***p < .001$. d = Effect size.

For evaluation 3 (appropriate rhythm and accent), a two-way ANOVA was conducted in which the dependent variables were the CNRep scores collected for evaluation 3 (Table 5), and the independent variables were the grade and number of syllables. ANOVA results identified significant main effects for grade and number of syllables [grade: $F(6, 258) = 6.98$, $p < .001$, $\eta^2 = .07$; number of syllables: $F(2.78, 717.88) = 176.90$, $p < .001$, $\eta^2 = .19$]. Interaction between grade and number of syllables was also significant [$F(16.70, 717.88) = 2.10$, $p = .006$, $\eta^2 = .01$].

Table 5. Two-way ANOVA of effects of school grade and number of syllables (Evaluation 3)

Source	df	SS	MS	F	p		η^2
Between Subjects							
Grades	6	7.17	1.20	6.98	<.001	***	.07
Error	258	44.18	0.17				
Within Subjects							
The number of syllables	2.78	19.37	6.96	176.90	<.001	***	.19
The number of syllables x Grades	16.70	1.38	0.08	2.10	.006	**	.01
Error (The number of syllables)	717.88	28.25	0.04				
Total	1001.36	100.35					

Note. $**p < .01$. $***p < .001$. η^2 = Effect size.

As a post hoc analysis, a Bonferroni adjustment was conducted (Table 6). The results were almost identical to those for evaluation 2, and they show that many syllable combinations were significant. Table 6 also shows comparison differences between numbers of neighboring syllables. Testing the participants on a small number of syllables revealed higher prosodic awareness and production with appropriate rhythm and accent. In contrast, as the number of syllables increased, participants across grades faced difficulty pronouncing sounds corresponding to the rhythm and accent of spoken English. As with the results from evaluation 2, only seventh-graders showed no significant differences for the number of syllables, except in four- and five-syllable comparisons, which is possibly attributable to differences in verbal STM capacities across grades. In addition to different cognitive development levels, results of prosody, such as rhythm and accent, were more likely caused by differences in rhythms between English (stress-based) and Japanese (mora-based) (Cutler & Otake, 1994, 2002) and the accent between English (high pitch on the accented syllable) and Japanese (high-low pitch). Therefore, the heavier the cognitive burden (many syllables in nonwords) and the more difficulty learners have in reproduction, the more likely there is to be an L1 negative transfer influence. This is especially pertinent for lower-grade participants who have not yet developed their cognitive abilities and have less knowledge of and exposure to English. Moreover, negative L1 transfer may have influenced the participants' poor performance in other tasks, such as phonological awareness during phonological analysis, retention of phonological representations in phonological storage, and production of correct output during speech motor planning.

Table 6. Post hoc analysis Bonferroni adjustment for evaluation 3

Evaluation	Grade	2 vs. 3 p	d	2 vs. 4 p	d	2 vs. 5 p	d	3 vs. 4 p	d	3 vs. 5 p	d	4 vs. 5 p	d
3	1	.002 **	0.47	<.001 ***	1.13	<.001 ***	1.45	<.001 ***	0.64	<.001 ***	0.96	.028 *	0.31
	2	<.001 ***	0.77	<.001 ***	0.75	<.001 ***	1.22	1.000	<0.01	.020 **	0.48	.007 **	0.47
	3	.003 **	0.61	<.001 ***	1.61	<.001 ***	1.85	<.001 ***	0.84	<.001 ***	1.16	.005 **	0.41
	4	.016 **	0.34	<.001 ***	1.03	<.001 ***	1.48	<.001 ***	0.70	<.001 ***	1.18	<.001 ***	0.55
	5	<.001 ***	0.72	<.001 ***	0.68	<.001 ***	1.76	1.000	<0.01	<.001 ***	1.02	<.001 ***	0.96
	6	<.001 ***	0.62	<.001 ***	0.94	<.001 ***	1.54	.010 **	0.33	<.001 ***	0.92	<.001 ***	0.58
	7	.391	0.28	.075	0.63	<.001 ***	1.08	.268	0.39	.001 ***	0.93	.005 **	0.67

Note. *p < .05. **p < .01. ***p < .001. d = Effect size.

Prosodic examinations showed similar features in evaluations 2 and 3, the main feature being difficulty in producing nonwords with many syllables, which was evident even for seventh-graders with the highest cognitive development. Tables 4 and 6 show that four-syllable nonwords may represent a threshold level in phonological processing, phonological production, and verbal STM. This suggests that the phonological analytic capacity of WM resources is overloaded and no resources remain to retain the original stimulus and reproduce it when there is greater phonological input.

RQ2 involved the influence of grade on prosodic reproduction of the number of syllables, rhythm, accent, and consonant clusters of EFL nonwords based on number of syllables. First, grade-level influence differed depending on the number of syllables in EFL nonwords. Although both grade level and number of syllables were involved in exact recall of the number of syllables, a grade difference was observed. Second, grade-level influence on appropriate rhythm and accent differed depending on the number of syllables. Although the number of syllables and grade were involved in the participants' ability to recall the appropriate rhythm and accent, grade-level influence differed according to the number of syllables. However, the influence of grade on clear consonant clusters did not differ according to the number of syllables because of the floor effect of lower scores.

Therefore, the answer to RQ2 is that prosodies, such as correspondence with number of syllables and appropriate rhythm and accent, were significantly influenced by grade and number of syllables; however, a fixed answer for consonant clusters could not be obtained because of the floor effect. There are two reasons for differing grade influences on the number of syllables in evaluations 2 and 3. The first is related to the cognitive development of verbal STM capacity and the second to differences in vocabulary size in LTM resulting from different levels of English exposure. However, a four-syllable barrier existed for all grades. The results from evaluation 1 (exact repetition) can be compared to those of Yuzawa et al. (2012), whose investigation of EFL children in an international kindergarten found that scores for two- to four-syllable nonwords for children aged four to six years were equal to, or better than, those of native English children. Yuzawa et al. (2012) interpreted lower EFL CNRep scores as reflecting negative transfer from L1 (Japanese).

4.4. Wordlikeness

Evaluation 1 differed significantly between high and low wordlikeness (Table 7), with high wordlikeness scores being considerably higher in all grades ($p < .001$) except the second ($p = .244$). It is assumed that high wordlikeness nonwords can be repeated more easily than low wordlikeness nonwords, although participants had difficulty in producing nonwords exactly (Table 1).

Table 7. Results of t-test for wordlikeness of CNRep for evaluations 1 to 3

Grade	df	Evaluation 1			Evaluation 2			Evaluation 3		
		t	p	d	t	p	d	t	p	d
1	33	4.03	<.001 ***	0.40	4.03	<.001 ***	0.42	1.44	.159	0.18
2	26	1.19	.244	0.23	3.47	<.001 ***	0.51	-0.16	.876	0.03
3	44	5.22	<.001 ***	0.58	7.52	<.001 ***	1.05	1.55	.128	0.22
4	53	7.17	<.001 ***	0.73	6.35	<.001 ***	0.82	1.40	.167	0.14
5	43	5.67	<.001 ***	0.78	7.52	<.001 ***	0.81	-1.12	.270	0.14
6	42	5.07	<.001 ***	0.73	7.07	<.001 ***	0.73	1.23	.224	0.14
7	17	5.25	<.001 ***	1.02	3.94	<.001 ***	0.95	-1.88	.077	0.45

Note. ***$p < .001$. d = Effect size. Evaluation 1, exact repetition; Evaluation 2, correspondence with the number of syllables; Evaluation 3, appropriate rhythm and accent.

For local phonological features in the two prosodic evaluations (2 and 3), average proportions were as follows. In evaluation 2, high wordlikeness ($p < .001$) produced higher scores across all grades, but there were no significant differences ($p > .05$) in evaluation 3.

For English nonwords with high and low wordlikeness, significant differences emerged in evaluations 1 and 2, but not 3, although this study's average for CNRep repetition was much lower than for young L1 children.

Given processes contributing to nonword reproduction, it is assumed that the limited vocabulary and LTM phonological knowledge of Japanese EFL students make it difficult for them to recognize and represent nonwords with different phonotactics from Japanese during phonological analysis, especially rhythm, accent, and consonant clusters, regardless of whether words have a high or low wordlikeness. In addition, during speech motor planning, if poorly stored phonological representations of words are degraded before retrieval then primed lexical representations can be used in the reintegration process to fill in missing information. However, because these students had few primed lexical representations, they had difficulty in compensating with their LTM for the missing rhythm, accent, and consonant cluster information.

5. Conclusion

This study highlighted two main findings regarding phonological features of verbal STM in Japanese EFL learners in foreign language activities at elementary school. First, phonological awareness and speech reproduction (repeating English nonwords accurately) macro-levels were more difficult for this study's participants than for L1 and L2 speakers who attended international or immersion schools and had considerably greater exposure to English. Furthermore, higher-grade students could repeat English nonwords better than lower-grade students due to differences in cognitive development (verbal STM capacities) and English language exposure. Second, phonological awareness and speech production differed depending on micro-levels, such as prosodies. Scores for accurate number of syllables, and appropriate rhythm and accent, were significantly higher for low numbers of syllables than for high numbers of syllables, except for seventh-graders. Seventh-graders had larger verbal STM capacities and greater exposure to English; they could therefore cope with a higher number of syllables. However, for consonant clusters, floor effects were observed across all grades because of a strong negative transfer from L1 (Japanese).

The teaching content and school curriculum examined here were almost identical to the present course of study in elementary school foreign language activities in Japan. Therefore, this study's findings have pedagogical implications for current foreign language activities in Japan.

Based on the findings discussed above, effects at the micro level of phonological English information, as seen in elementary school foreign language activities, may be related to the macro level of phonological English information (e.g., reading aloud, listening, speaking), and be emphasized in phonological English learning as a subject. If a micro-unit of information cannot be heard during auditory processing, and phonotactic frequency is based on the listeners' phonological awareness during phonological analysis, it is impossible to retain phonological representations in phonological storage to produce a macro-unit of language during speech motor planning.

This study considered phonological features (four evaluations), language familiarity (superiority of high-rated over low-rated wordlikeness), exposure to English, cognitive development (STM capacities in each academic grade), and information quantity (number of syllables). Pedagogical implications for teaching spoken English can be drawn from the results.

First, when Japanese EFL learners are taught English pronunciation, they have difficulty in attaining native-speaker-like pronunciation and pronouncing consonant clusters because of negative transfer from L1 Japanese, despite having taken many English lessons. Exposure to spoken English, through language activities, may affect phonological learning at the micro-level, such as prosodic features (syllables, rhythms, and accents).

Second, significant differences emerged between high- and low-rated wordlikeness; all participants except second-graders could repeat high-rated wordlikeness stimuli more exactly than low-rated stimuli in evaluation 1 (exact repetition) and evaluation 2 (correspondence with number of syllables). These language-familiarity effects, apart from appropriate rhythm, accent, and clear consonant clusters, are influenced by English vocabulary and phonological knowledge, and may reflect the effects of exposure to spoken English in English lessons.

Third, in English lessons, if lower-grade students are given words with many syllables (four or more) over a limited period, the task is likely to be beyond their verbal STM processing ability, resulting in inefficient lessons. Therefore, students should be exposed to English information in smaller units of fewer than four syllables so as not to exhaust their limited verbal STM resources.

Finally, owing to the higher cognitive burden of pronouncing words with more than four syllables, repeated practice is necessary, even for students in the highest grades, and even for those with more exposure to English and those at higher levels of cognitive development. Providing such repetition may enable EFL learners to improve their English phonological information processing efficiency in verbal STM for words with a higher number of syllables.

This study presented only basic data on phonological features of verbal STM in first- to sixth-graders who had participated in English activities, and in seventh-graders who had begun to study English as a subject. Since most previous studies of L1 and EFL have been based on formal instruction, future research should include a similar basis so as to be comparable.

The introduction of significant changes to Japanese English language education by the academic year 2020 is necessary. MEXT is considering the following changes. It is investigating whether to offer English language activities to third- and fourth-graders using the same methods as presently used for fifth- and sixth-graders; the aim is to familiarize younger students only with spoken English while under the new curriculum, while for fifth- and sixth-graders English lessons would focus on the acquisition of explicit linguistic knowledge through written English, in addition to spoken English. These dramatic changes in the elementary school curriculum may encourage more EFL learners to study English consciously and diligently, not only at school but also out of school, for instance, at private language schools.

Therefore, future research should examine the various purposes of English language learning for elementary students. These could include, not only gaining familiarity with basic spoken English but also learning explicit English forms, such as spelling and lexis with increased syllables as well as grammar, and exposing students to various types of English lessons, including activities and English as a subject, such as in immersion programs or international schools. Furthermore, future research should consider a cross-sequential study, ranging from first to sixth grades, with more participants and varying English proficiency levels.

Acknowledgements

The author would like to thank the teachers and students who cooperated with this research, and also Professor Shuichi Takaki for his valuable comments.

References

Avons, S. E., Wragg, C. A., Cupples, W. L., & Lovegrove, W. J. (1998). Measures of phonological short-term memory and their relationship to vocabulary development. *Applied Psycholinguistics, 19*(4), 583–601. doi.org/10.1017/S0142716400010377

Baddeley, A. D., Gathercole, S. E., & Papagno, C. (1998). The phonological loop as a language learning device. *Psychological Review, 105*(1), 158–173.

Baddeley, A. D., Allen, R. J., & Hitch, G. J. (2011). Binding in visual working memory: The role of the episodic buffer. *Neuropsychologia, 49*(6), 1393–1400. doi:10.1016/j.neuropsychologia.2010.12.042

Chiat, S. & Roy, P. (2007). The preschool repetition test: An evaluation of performance in typically developing and clinically referred children. *Journal of Speech, Language, and Hearing Research, 50*(2), 429–443. doi:10.1044/1092-4388(2007/030)

Chincotta, D. & Hoosain, R. (1995). Reading rate, articulatory suppression and bilingual digit span. *European Journal of Cognitive Psychology, 7*(2), 201–211. doi:10.1080/09541449508403100

Chincotta, D. & Underwood, G. (1996). Mother tongue, language of schooling and bilingual digit span. *British Journal of Psychology, 87*(2), 193–208. doi:10.1111/j.2044-8295.1996.tb02585.x

Chincotta, D. & Underwood, G. (1997). Bilingual memory span advantage for Arabic numerals over digit words. *British Journal of Psychology, 88*(2), 295–310. doi:10.1111/j.2044-8295.1997.tb02636.x

Cutler, A. & Otake, T. (1994). Mora or phoneme? Further evidence for language-specific listening. *Journal of Memory and Language, 33*(6), 824–844. doi:10.1006/jmla.1994.1039

Cutler, A. & Otake, T. (2002). Rhythmic categories in spoken-word recognition. *Journal of Memory and Language, 46*(2), 296–322. doi:10.1006/jmla.2001.2814

da Costa Pinto, A. (1991). Reading rates and digit span in bilinguals: The superiority of mother tongue. *International Journal of Psychology, 26*(4), 471–483. doi:10.1080/00207599108247135

Gathercole, S. E. (2006). Nonword repetition and word learning: The nature of the relationship. *Applied Psycholinguistics, 27*(4), 513–543. doi.org/10.1017/S0142716406060383

Gathercole, S. E. & Alloway, T. P. (2008). *Working memory & learning: A practical guide for teachers*. London: SAGE.

Gathercole, S. E. & Baddeley, A. D. (1989). Evaluation of the role of phonological STM in the development of vocabulary in children: A longitudinal study. *Journal of Memory and Language, 28*(2), 200–213. doi:10.1016/0749-596X(89)90044-2

Gathercole, S. E. & Baddeley, A. D. (1996). *The children's test of nonword repetition*. London, UK: Psychological.

Gathercole, S. E., Hitch, G. J., Service, E., & Martin, A. J. (1997). Phonological short-term memory and new word learning in children. *Developmental Psychology, 33*(6), 966–979. doi.org/10.1037/0012-1649.33.6.966

Gathercole, S. E., Willis, C. S., Baddeley, A. D., & Emslie, H. (1994). The children's test of nonword repetition: A test of phonological working memory. *Memory, 2*(2), 103–127. doi:10.1080/09658219408258940

Gathercole, S. E., Willis, C. S., Emslie, H., & Baddeley, A. D. (1991). The influences of number of syllables and wordlikeness on children's repetition of nonwords. *Applied Psycholinguistics, 12*(3), 349–367. doi.org/10.1017/S0142716400009267

Li, S., Yuzawa, M., & Sekiguchi M. (2009). Nihongo bogo yoji to chugokugo bogo yoji ni okeru eigo onin shori no chigai. [Differences in phonological processing of English words by Japanese and Chinese preschoolers]. *The Japanese Journal of Developmental Psychology, 20*(3), 289–298. http://ci.nii.ac.jp/naid/110007360390/en

Masoura, E. V. & Gathercole, S. E. (1999). Phonological short-term memory and foreign vocabulary learning. *International Journal of Psychology, 34*(5-6), 383-388. doi:10.1080/002075999399738

Masoura, E. V. & Gathercole, S. E. (2005). Phonological short-term memory skills and new word learning in young Greek children. *Memory, 13*(3/4), 422-429.

Michas, I. C. & Henry, L. A. (1994). The link between phonological memory and vocabulary acquisition. *British Journal of Developmental Psychology, 12*(2), 147-164. doi:10.1111/j.2044-835X.1994.tb00625.x

Ministry of Education, Culture, Sports, Science and Technology [MEXT]. (2008). *Shogakko gakushu shido youryo gaikokugo katsudo hen* [Course of study for foreign language activities in elementary school] Tokyo: Toyokan Shuppansha.

Munson, B., Kurtz, B. A., & Windsor, J. (2005). The influence of vocabulary size, phonotactic probability, and wordlikeness on nonword repetitions of children with and without language impairments. *Journal of Speech, Language, and Hearing Research, 48*(5), 1033-1047. doi:10.1044/1092-4388(2005/072)

Roy, P. & Chiat, S. (2004). A prosodically controlled word and nonword repetition task for 2- to 4-year-olds: Evidence from typically developing children. *Journal of Speech, Language, and Hearing Research, 47*, 223-234. doi:10.1044/1092-4388(2004/019)

Sakuma, Y. (2011). Cognitive features of working memory in elementary school students participating in foreign language activities. *Annual Review of English Language Education, 22*, 233-248. http://ci.nii.ac.jp/naid/110009425259

Sakuma Y. & Saito, S. (2012). The positive influence of English-language activities on English digit-span performance among Japanese elementary school children: A three-year cross-sequential study. *Psychologia: An International Journal of Psychological Sciences, 55*(4), 257-268. doi.org/10.2117/psysoc.2012.257

Service, E. (1992). Phonology, working memory, and foreign-language learning. *Quarterly Journal of Experimental Psychology, 45*(1), 21-50. doi:10.1080/14640749208401314

Service, E. & Kohonen, V. (1995). Is the relation between phonological memory and foreign-language learning accounted for by vocabulary acquisition? *Applied Psycholinguistics, 16*(2), 155-172. doi.org/10.1017/S0142716400007062

Thorn, A. S. C. & Gathercole, S. E. (1999). Language-specific knowledge and short-term memory in bilingual and non-bilingual children. *The Quarterly Journal of Experimental Psychology, 52*(2), 303-324. doi:10.1080/713755823

Thorn, A. S. C. & Gathercole, S. E. (2001). Language differences in verbal short-term memory do not exclusively originate in the process of subvocal rehearsal. *Psychonomic Bulletin & Review, 8*(2), 357–364. doi:10.3758/BF03196173

Thorn, A. S. C., Gathercole, S. E., & Frankish, C. R. (2002). Language familiarity effects in short-term memory: The role of output delay and long-term knowledge. *Quarterly Journal of Experimental Psychology Section A, 55*(4), 1363–1383. doi:10.1080/02724980244000198

Thorn, A. S. C. (2005). Redintegration and the benefits of long-term knowledge in verbal short-term memory: An evaluation of Schweikert's (1993) multinomial processing tree model. *Cognitive Psychology, 50*(2), 133–158. doi:10.1016/j.cogpsych.2004.07.001

Vitevitch, M. S. & Luce, P. A. (2005). Increases in phonotactic probability facilitate spoken nonword repetition. *Journal of Memory and Language, 52*(2), 193–204. doi:10.1016/j.jml.2004.10.003

Yamaguchi, A., Shimizu, M., Hijikata, Y., & Imai, S. (2013). *Immersion kyoiku wo ukeru nihonjin chugakusei no oninteki sadokioku ni kansuru kenkyu.* [The phonological working memory of Japanese students at an English immersion junior high school: Using a nonword repetition task]. Gunma Daigaku Kyoiku Jissen Kenkyu (Research in educational practice and development, Gunma University), *30*, 199–209. https://gair.media.gunma-u.ac.jp/dspace/handle/10087/7490

Yuzawa, Miki & Saito, S. (2006). The role of prosody and long-term phonological knowledge in Japanese children's nonword repetition performance. *Cognitive Development, 21*(2), 146–157. doi:10.1016/j.cogdev.2006.01.003

Yuzawa, Masamichi, Yuzawa, Miki, Sekiguchi, M., & Li, S. (2012). *Nihonjin yoji ni okeru eigo onin shutoku noryoku: eigo hitango hanpuku ni yoru kento.* [Young Japanese children's ability to acquire English sounds: Examination by English nonword repetition]. *The Japanese Journal of Educational Psychology, 60*(1), 60–69. https://www.jstage.jst.go.jp/article/jjep/60/1/60_60/_article

外国語として英語を学習している日本人の小学1年生から中学1年生における言語性短期記憶の音韻的特徴

佐久間康之（福島大学）

要旨

　本研究は、発話された英語の言語性短期記憶における音韻的特徴に焦点を当てて日本の小学校における英語活動の効果を調査した。小学1年生から中学1年生（265名）は英語の非単語反復課題を受けた。教育的示唆を含め主に4点を報告している。第一に母語からの負の干渉により、非単語を正確に発音できる学習者や非単語内の子音連結を発音できる学習者はいなかった。第二に、小学2年生を除く全学年において、非単語の正確な反復に音節数が関与すると思われる単語らしさの高低による言語親密性効果に関して有意差があった。第三に、全ての学習者は音韻情報が4音節を超えるとその情報を保持し産出することが困難であった。この点は小学生以上に繰り返し訓練を受けてきた中学1年生でさえも同様であった。これらの結果は、学年の低い学習者ほど言語性短期記憶が小さいため、この有限な認知資源を消費し尽してしまわないように4音節よりも少ない英語情報に接触させるべきであることを明らかにしている。

文法指導の順序に関する実証的研究：中国語の動詞接辞"了1"と文末助詞"了2"に焦点を当てて

許　挺傑（大分県立芸術文化短期大学）
鈴木祐一（神奈川大学）
劉　驫（九州大学）

要旨

　本研究の目的は、第二言語の文法の指導順序を変えることの影響を明らかにすることである。日本語を母語とする中国語学習者を対象にして、動詞接辞"了1"を先に教えた場合と、文末助詞"了2"を先に教えた場合では、どのように習得過程が異なるか検証した。パイロット実験で日本語母語話者にとって、"了2"の方が"了1"よりも習得が難しいということを示した。そして、本実験では文法習得難易度の異なる"了1"と"了2"の指導順序を、実際の大学の授業で変えることで、それぞれの習得にどのような影響を与えるか調べた。結果、受容的知識に関しては、指導順序を変えても、習得には大きな影響が見られなかった一方、産出的知識に関しては、後に教えられた"了"の方が、習得が高まる結果が示唆された。表層的には同じ形式である"了"の2つの用法の指導順序を変えても、様々な要因が習得に影響し、"了1"と"了2"の指導順序が与える影響というのは、限定的であると現段階では考えられる。

1. 序章

　第二言語教育において、同じ形式だが複数の意味を持つ文法項目があった場合、どの意味用法から先に教えたら良いのかという指導順序に関してよく議論されることがある。しかし、どちらの意味用法を教えたほうが効果的なのかということを、実証的に調べた研究は少ない (Eckman, Bell, & Nelson, 1988; Ishida, 2004; Ryu & Shirai, 2011)。本研究では、中国語の動詞接辞の"了"（以下、了1) と文末助詞の"了"（以下、了2) に着目し、指導順序の効果検証を行う。

　"了1"と"了2"の文法的意味機能について、すでに数多くの先行研究において議論がなされているが、"了1"は「動作の完了」を表し、"了2"は「状況の変化」を表すという説が多くの研究者から支持されている（呂, 1999; 木村, 1997, 2012）。そして、日本国内におけるほとんどの初級中国語教科書もこの説明を採用しているため、本研究もこの定義に従う。"了1"と"了2"は、表層形式は同じであるが、異なる意味を表し、習得の難易度が異なると考えられている。このように習得の難易度が異なる文法項目の指導順序を、教室で変えることで、文法習得を促進できるかどうかを検証することは、教育的な示唆を得られることに加え、習得のメカニズムを解明するという理論的な貢献もある（白井, 2002）。本研究では、日本語母語話者を対象として、"了1"を先に教えた場合と、"了2"を先に教えた場合では、どのように習得過程が異なるか検証する。

2. 先行研究
2.1. 文法学習における指導順序の効果

特定の文法項目の指導順序が第二言語習得に影響をどう与えるか調べた研究は主にプロジェクション・モデルの枠組みで行われてきた（Zobl, 1983, 1985）。プロジェクション・モデルは、ある言語理論の中で"有標"とされる相対的に難しい文法項目を先に教えると、無標の文法項目の習得が促進されると予測する。つまり、より難しい有標の文法項目を学習したことから、より簡単な無標の文法項目の学習へ応用することができる可能性が示されている。本論文では、有標・無標ということの定義に関して詳細に議論しないが、代表的な研究の例として、Eckman et al.（1988）を紹介する。

彼らの実験では、第二言語として英語を学習する学生に対して、関係節の指導を行なった。Noun phrase accessibility hierarchy（Keenan & Comrie, 1977）に基づいて、有標度の異なる 3 種類の関係節が選ばれた。有標度の低い順番から、① 主格関係節（e.g., John likes the professor who gives easy exams to the class.）、② 目的格関係節（e.g., Janet rode the bicycle which your father gave to Jim.）、そして最も有標な ③ 前置詞を伴う目的格関係節（e.g., The chairman listened to the student to whom the professor gave a low grade）が指導の対象となった。実験では、3 つの実験群に分けられ、それぞれの群では、上記の 3 つの関係節のうち一つだけが教えられた。結果、③ だけを教えられた群は、① と ② の習得も進むことが明らかにされた。一方、① か ② だけを教えられた群では、より有標な文法項目の学習は促進されないことが分かった。この結果は、指導順序が習得に影響することを示している。しかし、プロジェクション・モデルが適用できる文法項目は限られており（e.g., Zobl, 1985; 秋葉、堀江、白井、2010）、プロジェクション・モデルの枠組み以外から、他の文法項目でも指導順序の効果検証を行うことができる可能性を探ることが重要だと考えられる（白井、2002）。

一つの方向性として、文法の表層形式は同じだが複数の異なる意味と習得難易度を示す文法項目の指導順序に関して調べる可能性が考えられる（Ishida, 2004; Ryu & Shirai, 2011）。Ryu and Shirai（2011）は、韓国語の非完結相（imperfective aspect）を表す形態素の指導順序を変えることが習得にどのように影響するかを調べた。韓国語の iss には、「進行」の意味を表す用法（-ko iss-）と「結果」の意味を表す用法（-ko iss/-a iss-）の 2 つがある。そして、「進行」用法が、「結果」用法よりも先に習得されることが分かっている（Lee & Kim, 2007; Ryu, Horie, & Shirai, 2015）。Ryu and Shirai は、韓国語を第二言語として教えている教室環境において、より難しいとされる「結果」用法を先に教える群（結果群）と、「進行」用法を先に教える群（進行群）の 2 群を比べた。結果、産出テストでは、両群に差はなかったものの、理解テストでは、結果群の方が進行群よりも平均点が高かった。ただし、理解テストでは合計 33 名を統計分析にかけているが、産出テストでは分析対象が 16 名と少なかった。このような研究方

法上の問題から、理解と産出過程の違いによって、指導の効果が変わるかどうかは分からない。しかし、Ryu and Shirai の研究結果は、同じ形式で異なる用法を持つ文法項目の指導順序を変えることで、習得を促進できる可能性を示している点で重要であろう。

2.2. 日本語母語話者の"了"の習得に関する研究
　本研究は、中国語における了の2つの用法に焦点を当てて、指導順序の効果を検証する。"了1"は、動詞の直後に置かれ、動作の完了を表す。

（1）我买了一本书。
　　 私は本を一冊買った。

　一方、"了2"は文末に置かれ、変化を表す。話者の視点や考えなどにより、様々な変化の意味を表すが、本研究ではその中でも、例（2）にあるように、初級中国語学習者にとって最も一般的な用法「変化」の意味に焦点を当てる。

（2）叶子红了。
　　 葉っぱが赤くなった。

　文法指導順序の効果を調べる上で、今回の"了1"と"了2"を選んだ理由は主に2点ある。第1に、一つの形式が複数の意味用法を表す項目は、他の意味－形式のマッピング（e.g., one-to-one form-meaning mapping）に比べて習得が難しいとされる。具体的には、第二言語学習者は、一つの形式には一つの意味だけを関連付けようとしてしまい、習得が困難になることが報告されている（Andersen, 1984; Clark, 1987）。
　第2の理由は、"了1"と"了2"が異なる"文法習得難易度"（"grammatical difficulty", Yalcin & Spada, 2016）を持っていると考えられるからである。この2つの項目は、同じ形で関連した意味用法を持ち合わせているが、特に日本語母語話者が学ぶ際に母語からの転移（first language transfer）が、習得難易度に影響すると考えられる。まず、完了を表す"了1"は、日本語の漢字の知識（e.g., 完了、終了）から、習得が簡単であると考えられる。一方、"了2"の表す「変化」の意味は、日本語の「了」という漢字には含意されていない。日本語母語話者にとって、日本語と中国語の漢字が共通していることから、"了1"を、完了を表す形態素「－た」と結びつけることが容易であると予測できる。一方、"了2"に関しては、日本語では「変化」の意味を表さないため、全く新しい形式と意味のマッピングを行う必要がある。特に、「"了1"＝完了」だという1対1対応が強く作られてしまうと、"了2"の習得が遅れてしまうのではないかと指摘されている（荒川, 2010, p. 1）。そのため、日本語母語話者にとっては、"了1"に比べて、"了2"の習得は困難な可能性がある。

"了1"と"了2"の習得の困難度は、漢字の形態的な類似度からの転移に加えて、語順規則の難易度にも影響を受けると考えられる。"了2"は、必ず文末に置かれるため、動詞の後ろに置かれた結果、文の様々な場所に現れる"了1"よりも、より簡単な規則であると考えられる。そのため、形態的な類似度による予測とは反対に、"了2"の方が"了1"よりも習得が容易だと予測することができる。

　以上の2つの要因（母語からの転移と語順規則）が、日本語母語話者にとって、"了1"と"了2"の習得に大きな影響を与えると考えられるが、"了1"と"了2"の文法習得難易度は実証的に十分に調べられているとは言えない。そのため、パイロット実験として、日本語母語話者を対象に、"了1"と"了2"の最も一般的な用法の習得状況を調べ、"了1"と"了2"の難易度を比較した。パイロット実験の目的は、"了1"と"了2"の習得の難易度を明らかにし、本実験（指導順序の効果検証）の計画と結果を実証的にサポートするために行なった。パイロット実験の結果、"了1"と"了2"の典型的な用法の場合、"了2"の方が"了1"よりも難しいことが支持された（詳細は第3章のパイロット実験参照）。

2.3. "了1"と"了2"の指導順序に関する議論

　"了1"と"了2"の指導順序に関しては、中国語教育の分野で山崎（2010）と荒川（2010）が議論している。山崎（2010）は、入門用教科書によく見られる指導順序を概観した上で、「同時導入」、"了2"→"了1"、"了1"→"了2"の3種類の導入パターンについて論じている。山崎氏によると、同時導入の場合、1課の中で2つの"了"を両方とも身につけさせるのは難しいと指摘している。そして、"了1"と"了2"をそれぞれ別の課で導入する場合、指導順序について、"了2"→"了1"のほうが、日本語話者にとって習得しやすい順序と指摘している(山崎, 2010, p. 76)。理由としては、"了2"は、必ず文末に置くということで、"了1"に比べて、統語的に簡単であるという点を挙げている。

　荒川（2010, p. 11）は、自編入門教科書（10種類）を分析した結果、"了1"と"了2"を同時に出すことが多かったが、別々に出すときは"了2"を先に出していると指摘した。荒川論文では、10種類の自編教科書しか対象としていないため、本研究では、より多くの初級中国語教科書でどのように"了1"と"了2"が提示されているかを調査した。日本で一般的に使われている初級教科書35冊を調べた結果、「同じ課での同時導入」が14冊、"了2"→"了1"が11冊、"了1"→"了2"が10冊であった。

　このように教科書ごとに提示の順番が異なる以上、実際にどのような提示順序で教えることが学習者にとって最も良いのか改めて考える必要があるであろう。その目的を達成するため、本研究は複数回の授業にわたり、"了1"と"了2"の指導順序の効果検証を行った。均一学習レベルの日本人中国語学習者を2つのグループに分け、一つのグループは"了1"→"了2"の順番で（「了1群」）、もう一つのグループは、"了2"→"了1"の順番で（「了2群」）それぞれ教えた。さらに、学習効果の測定を客観的に行うため、同質の問題文から成り立つ事前・

事後・遅延事後テストを用意し、3回のテストを行った（詳細は第3章の本実験参照）。

3. パイロット実験"了1"と"了2"の難易度に関する実験

パイロット実験は、"了1"と"了2"の最も一般的な用法の習得の難易度の推定を試みた。パイロット実験で"了1"と"了2"の習得の難易度を明らかにし、本実験（指導順序の効果検証）の研究計画、及び結果解釈に役立てようとした。

3.1. 実験参加者

実験参加者は、日本の大学における中国語専攻の学生であった（2年生18名［学習期間：1年6ヶ月］、3年生15名［学習期間：2年6ヶ月］、4年生16名［学習期間：3年6ヶ月］で計49名）。テストでは本実験の事前テストと全く同じ問題を利用した。

3.2. 文法項目

"了"にはさまざまな用法があるが、本実験の参加者が初級学習者であることに鑑みて、最も一般的な用法に限定した。まず、"了1"は、過去時制表現が動詞の前にあり、動詞の目的語の前に数量・時量表現が用いられ、"了"が動詞の直後につき、「完了」を表すものとした（例(3)）。確実に"了1"であると区別できるため、数量・時量表現を伴う"了1"に絞った。一方、"了2"に関しては、名詞・形容詞文と動詞文（否定文）の最後につき、「変化」を表す場合のみを扱った。名詞・形容詞文は、状態の変化を表し（例(4)）、動詞文（否定文）に関しては、心理の変化を表す（例(5)）。"了2"動詞文の中でも、否定文のみに絞った理由は、動詞文の肯定文だと、"了1"との区別ができなくなるためである。なお、すべての実験参加者は、同じ教科書（康玉華, 来思平 (2006)『中国語会話301（上・下）』（第3版）語文研究社）を使って、1年生の前期（第11課）に"了2"、後期（第22課）に"了1"について、学習済みである。

(3) "了1" 昨天我买了一件衣服。（昨日私は服を1着買いました）
(4) "了2" 我是大学生了。（私は大学生になりました）
(5) "了2" 我不去图书馆了。（私は図書館へ行くのをやめました）

3.3. テスト内容

意味解釈テストと和文中訳テストの2種類のテストを実施した。実験協力者のレベルを考えると、音声を使ったテストよりも文字による提示のテストの方が適切だと考えられるため、読みと書きのテストを選んだ。意味解釈テストは受容的知識、和文中訳テストは産出的知識を測るために用いた。なお、2種類のテスト実施の順番は、(1) 意味解釈テスト、(2) 和文中訳テストの順番にして、"了"を使用する際にその文法事項を意識する必要のある度合いが低いものか

らテストした。

3.3.1. 意味解釈テスト

意味解釈テストでは、"了"を含む中国語の単文とその日本語訳を提示して、中国語の文が日本語文の意味と一致しているかを判断してもらった。実験参加者には、日本語訳の文は常に正しいため、中国語の文が正しいかどうかを判断するように指示をした。

テスト問題には、"了1"と"了2"が完全に区別できる文を選んだ（6a, 7a）。また、中国語の"了1"と"了2"それぞれ、2種類の非文法的なエラーを用意した。"了"を使うべき所で使われていない文は脱落エラー文（6b, 7b）で、了の位置が"了1"と"了2"で逆になっている文は位置エラーとした（6c, 7c）。

(6) "了1"の例（「*」は非文を意味する）
    a. 星期三她上了3节课。（水曜日に彼女は3コマの授業を受けました）
    b. *昨天下午她买1条裤子。（昨日の午後彼女は1枚のズボンを買いました）
    c. *昨天早上我喝2杯茶了。（昨日の朝私は2杯のお茶を飲みました）

(7) "了2"の例
    a. 他是留学生了。（彼は留学生になりました）
    b. *她是大学生。（彼女は大学生になりました）
    c. *她不去了食堂。（彼女は食堂に行かないことにしました）

フィラー文として、既習の文法項目を含むものを用意した（例(8)(9)）。

(8) 正文の例　他没吃包子。（彼は肉まんを食べませんでした）
(9) 非文の例　*他们也去上海。（彼らはみんな上海に行きます）

テストでは、"了1"文、"了2"文、フィラー文の3種類の問題を、それぞれ8問ずつ作成した（8問×3種類＝24問）。それぞれの種類に関して、「正文」と「非文」を4問ずつ用意した。"了1"文と"了2"文の「非文」は、「位置」と「脱落」のエラーを含むものを半分ずつ（2問ずつ）用意した。

テスト問題はマイクロソフトのパワーポイントによって提示し、実験参加者は解答用紙に解答を記入した。了の知識を持った実験参加者が確実に解答できるように、1問ごとの解答制限時間を12秒に設定した[1]。単語はすべて実験参加者が学習したことのある既習語のみを用いた。テストの前に、例題を2問見せて、テストの内容を理解してもらった上で、テストを受けてもらった。

---

[1] パイロットテストの結果、制限時間を設定した。

3.3.2. 和文中訳テスト

　和文中訳テストは、日本語の文を中国語に訳してもらった。テストに用いた例文は(10)と(11)のようなものである。意味解釈テストと同様に、"了1"と"了2"、フィラー((8)と(9)と同種類)の3種類の問題を、それぞれ4問ずつで計12問用意した。テスト問題はマイクロソフトのパワーポイントによって提示し、実験参加者は解答用紙に解答を記入した。了の知識を持った実験参加者が確実に解答できるように、1問ごとの解答制限時間は1分20秒に設定した[2]。内容語などの知識の有無によって、"了"の解答に影響が出ないように、翻訳に必要な内容語はすべて与えた。

(10)　"了1"の例　午前中彼女は1冊の雑誌を買いました。(上午、本、雑誌、买)　→　(正解)上午、她买了一本杂志。
(11)　"了2"の例　彼女は病気になりました。(病)　→　(正解)她病了。

3.4. テストの採点基準

　意味解釈テストは、正解と不正解を採点した。和文中訳テストは、以下の採点基準を用いて採点を行った[3]。2つのテストの合計得点は、それぞれパーセンテージで算出した。

表1. 和文中訳テストの採点基準

① "了"を正しく使えた場合 → (1点)
② "了"が脱落した場合 → (0点)
③ "了"の位置が誤った場合 → (0点)
④ その他の誤り → (0点)

　①については、完璧な正解のほか、文中に"了"と関係のない1箇所誤りがあった場合は、その誤りは許容した。その文において"了"の使い方が正しければ正しいと見なした(例(12)と(13)、括弧内は正解)。

(12)　いま5時になりました。　→　现在5个了。(现在5点了)
(13)　彼女は病気になりました。　→　病了。(她病了)

---

[2] パイロットテストの結果、制限時間を設定した。
[3] 中国語母語話者である2名の著者が採点を行った。28枚の解答を用いて、2名の著者がまずそれぞれ独自に採点を行った。2名の採点結果の一致度は、94.64%(224問中212問一致)であった。その後、2名の採点結果が一致しなかった点に関して、議論を行い、採点基準の摺り合わせを行った。最終的には残りのすべての解答(パイロット実験と本実験合計180枚)は1名の中国語母語話者(2名のうちの一人)が行った。

②の脱落と③の位置の誤りについては、前文においてすでに例が挙げられている（脱落エラー（6b, 7b）、位置エラー（6c, 7c））。ここでは主に④の「その他の誤り」について説明する。

具体的には、目的語の位置が誤って、完了の"了1"か、変化の"了2"かが判別できない場合は、これを誤りとする。たとえば、実際の誤用例（14）（15）のように、語順がSVOでなく、SOVになっている場合は、"了"が語尾に置かれているが、"了1"か"了2"の区別がつかなくなってしまうため、誤りと見なした。

(14) 私はお酒を飲まないことにしました。→ 我酒喝了。（正解：我不喝酒了）
(15) 昨日の午後彼女は2コマの授業を受けました。→ 昨天下午她两课上节了。（正解：昨天下午她上了两节课）

このほか、解答欄が空欄に近かった場合も④「その他の誤り」と見なした。

3.5. 結果

表2にパイロット実験の意味解釈テストと和文中訳テストの結果を提示する。対応ありのノンパラメトリック検定であるWilcoxon signed-rank testを行なって、各学年ごとに"了1"と"了2"の正答率を比較した。

意味解釈テストに関しては、2年生と3年生では、"了1"と"了2"の問題の正答率に統計的に有意な差は見られなかった（$p > .05$）。しかし、4年生においては、"了2"の方が統計的に有意に正答率が低かった（$p = .02$）。

和文中訳テストにおいては、すべての学年において、"了2"の方が"了1"よりも統計的に有意に難しかった（$p < .05$）。以上の結果から、"了1"と"了2"の典型的な用法の場合、"了1"に比べ"了2"がより難しいと推測できる。この結果は荒川（2010: 1）を支持するものであった。

表2. "了1"と"了2"の難易度テストの結果

		了1		了2			
	N	M	SD	M	SD	z	p
意味解釈テスト							
2年生	18	67.50	21.50	64.00	21.78	-0.76	.45
3年生	15	80.07	15.74	80.00	16.40	-0.12	.91
4年生	16	82.88	13.81	68.69	19.92	-2.42	.02
和文中訳テスト							
2年生	18	77.78	30.78	52.78	24.08	-2.34	.02
3年生	15	90.00	18.42	71.67	29.68	-2.05	.04
4年生	16	90.63	17.97	71.88	28.69	-2.22	.03

注：N=人数、M=平均値、SD=標準偏差。

そして、教育上特に重要な問題になるのは、より簡単な"了1"を先に教える場合と、より難しい"了2"を先に教える場合では、それぞれの習得にどのような違いが出るのかということである。次章の本実験では、"了1"と"了2"の指導順序の効果に関する研究を報告する。

4. 本実験"了1"と"了2"の指導順序に関する実験

本実験では、"了1"と"了2"の指導順序を変えることで、それぞれの習得にどのような影響を与えるか実証的に調べる。参加者は、パイロット実験の実験参加者とは異なる学習者であった。

4.1. 実験参加者

実験参加者は日本の大学の1年生対象の中国語授業（2015年度後期開講）の日本語母語話者104名の受講者であった。中国語学習経験は、2015年度前期に開講された授業（4月から8月まで）での学習経験があるだけで、初級レベルであった。104名の学生は、学籍番号順に2クラス（51名と53名）に分かれており、一つのクラスは、"了1"から教える「了1群」として、もう一方は"了2"から教える「了2群」とした。授業は、著者の一人である中国語担当の教員がすべて行った。また、授業の欠席等の関係で、"了"の指導に関するすべての授業に参加した学生のみを分析対象とした。そのため、最終的に分析対象となった学生の数は、「了1群」と「了2群」、それぞれ28名と25名となった。

4.2. 指導教材と手順

この節では、指導に使用した教材と指導手順について説明する。具体的な文法項目に関してはパイロット実験の3.2節を参照されたい。指導は通常の90分授業の一部（20〜30分程度）を実験に当てた。両群とも指導内容は全く同じであるが、「了1群」では、"了1"→"了2"、「了2群」では"了2"→"了1"という順序で、順序のみを変えて指導を行った。具体的な実施スケジュールは以下の図1の通りである。

	「了1群」	「了2群」
Day1（第1週）	事前テスト	
Day2（第2週）	(A) "了1"の文法説明と練習1（30分）	(D) "了2"の文法説明と練習1（30分）
	↓	↓
Day3（第4週）	(B) "了1"の練習2（30分）	(E) "了2"の練習2（30分）
	↓	↓
Day4（第5週）	(C) "了1"の復習（5分） (D) "了2"の文法説明と練習1（30分）	(F) "了2"の復習（5分） (A) "了1"の文法説明と練習1（30分）
	↓	↓
Day5（第7週）	(E) "了2"の練習2（30分）	(B) "了1"の練習2（30分）
	↓	↓
Day6（第8週）	(F) "了2"の復習（5分）	(C) "了1"の復習（5分）
Day7（第9週）	事後テスト	
Day8（第12週）	遅延事後テスト	

図1. 指導の手順

　指導は、12週間にわたり、8日間行った。Day1に事前テストを行い、その次の週から5日間（7週間）にわたり、"了1"と"了2"の指導を行った。Day4では、一方の"了"の復習（CまたはF）を簡単に行ってから、他方の"了"の導入（DまたはA）を行った。なお、第3週と第6週は、"了"に関する授業は行わなかった（休校のため）。第8週（Day6）が"了"に関する授業の最後で、その1週間後に事後テストを行い、事後テストからさらに3週間後、指導の効果がどれくらい持続されているかを測定するため、遅延事後テストを第12週に行った。以上のように、1学期間にわたり、"了"の指導を行うことで、一方の"了"の用法をしっかりと理解させてから、もう一方の"了"の指導を行えるようにした。

　指導の手順は、"了1"も"了2"も同様に、(A/D)「"了"に関する文法説明と練習1」、(B/E)「"了"に関する練習2」、(C/F)「"了"に関する復習」というセットで行った。"了1"の指導を例として、(A)から(C)までの手順を説明する。

　まず、「(A) "了1"に関する文法説明と練習1」では、「"了1"なし」文を3文（例: 我买1件衣服／私は服を一着買います）と「"了1"あり」文を3文（例: 我买了1件衣服／私は服を一着買いました）を同時に提示して、どのように意味が異なるかを考えさせながら、"了1"の意味や用法、文内の位置、文の特徴などについて明示的な説明を行った（付録1）。そして、"了1"を使った2種類の練習を行った。日本語から中国語に訳す練習を4問（例(16)）と、中国語の質問文に中国語で答える準備をして、ペアでやり取りを5問行わせた（例(17)）（付録2）。

（16）今日私は2つのおにぎりを食べました。（饭团、吃、2个、今天）
（17）上星期，你学了多长时间汉语？（先週、あなたは中国語をどれぐらいの時間勉強しましたか？）

「(B)"了1"に関する練習2」では、例4と同様の和文中訳の問題（必要単語と絵を提示）を4問出し、練習させた（付録3）。「(C)"了1"に関する復習」では、「(B)"了1"に関する練習2」の問題の答え合わせという形で5分程度行った。以上のような(A)から(C)までの手順を、全く同じ形で、"了2"についても同様に指導を行った（付録4-6を参照）。

4.3. 事前・事後・遅延事後テスト

パイロット実験で使ったテストと同じ2種類のテストによって、実験参加者の"了1"と"了2"に関する知識を測定した。意味解釈テストで受容的知識を、和文中訳テストで産出的知識をそれぞれ測った。事前・事後・遅延事後テストは、同質の異なる文を作成した。

なお、パイロット実験で使った意味解釈テストは、本実験の事前テストと全く同じもので、一方、事後テストと遅延事後テストでは、"了1"と"了2"の問題の数を16問に増やし、フィラー問題の数はそのままの8問とした（16問×2種類＋8問＝40問）。文法性（文法的・非文法的）、エラーの種類（脱落・位置）の割合は半分ずつとした。事後テストに比べて、事前テストの問題数が少ないのは、実験参加者は"了"が未習であるということを確認することが主な目的だったため、実験参加者の負担を軽減する目的もあり、問題数を半分にした。

4.4. 結果
4.4.1. 意味解釈テストの結果

表3に意味解釈テストの結果を提示する。二択問題であったため、全く知識がない学習者であれば、事前テストの場合、平均値が50％近くになるはずであったが、予想通り、平均値は50％から60％であった。テストの信頼性（一貫性）を調べるために、クロンバックのα係数を算出した。事後テストでは了1が.88で、了2は.82であった。遅延事後テストでは、了1が.89で、了2が.84であった。事前テストでは、受験者は"了1"と"了2"を知らなかったため当て推量で答えたと考えられ、α係数は低かった（了1 = .26, 了2 = .06）。

表3. 意味解釈テストの結果

	事前		事後		遅延事後	
	M	SD	M	SD	M	SD
合計（了1＋了2）						
了1群	51.34	11.71	71.21	17.48	75.11	19.64
了2群	54.25	10.93	81.13	18.87	81.25	19.89
了1						
了1群	41.52	17.70	68.97	26.87	66.29	27.81
了2群	49.00	16.89	84.00	20.50	79.25	24.72
了2						
了1群	61.16	17.46	73.44	20.31	83.93	18.90
了2群	59.50	14.11	78.25	21.66	83.25	20.86

注：灰色のセルが指導からテストまでの間隔を揃えた上での比較対象となっている。

　まず、"了"の指導前の事前テストの結果において、「了1群」と「了2群」の間に得点の差がないかをMann–Whitney U testで比較した。事前テストの合計点数（"了1"と"了2"の合計）、"了1"のみの点数、"了2"のみの点数のすべてにおいて、「了1群」と「了2群」の間に統計的な有意な差は見られなかった（$p > .05$）。次に、事後テストと遅延事後テストの合計点を見てみると、「了2群」の方がわずかに「了1群」よりも得点が高いように見える。しかし、「了1群」と「了2群」の間の差を正確に見るためには、合計点を比べることには問題がある。なぜなら、両群の間に、指導からテストまでの間隔に差があるからである（図1参照）。「了1群」では、第5週に"了1"の指導が終わるが、「了2群」では、"了1"の指導の終わりは第8週である。そのため、指導から事後テストまでの期間は、「了1群」では4週間で、「了2群」では1週間となってしまう。そのため、指導とテストまでの間隔を揃えるために、"了1"の得点に関しては、「了1群」の事後テスト（"了1"の指導終了から4週間後）と「了2群」の遅延事後テスト（"了1"の指導終了から4週間後）を統計的に比較する。同様に、"了2"の得点に関しては、「了1群」の遅延事後テストと「了2群」の事後テストを比較する。以上のように、指導からテストまでの間隔を揃えた上で得点を比べることで、指導順序の効果を適切に評価することができる。

　まず、"了1"に関しては、「了1群」が68.97%で、「了2群」が79.25%であった。Mann–Whitney U testの結果、両群に統計的に有意な差はなかった、$U = 256.50$ (51) = 0.144, $p = .09$, $r = 0.23$。同様に、"了2"に関しては、「了1群」が83.93%で、「了2群」が78.25%であったが、統計的に有意な差は見られなかっ

た、$U = 298.50, p = .35, r = 0.13$。以上の結果から、意味解釈テストに関しては、両群において統計的に有意な差は見られなかったことになる。

4.4.2. 和文中訳テストの結果
　表 4 に和文中訳テストの結果を提示する。「了 1 群」のうち、1 名が事前テストにおいて、"了 1" の 1 問だけ正解し、同じ群の別の 1 名が "了 2" の 1 問だけを正解した。この 2 名は、残りの問題はすべて不正解であったため、たまたま正解した問題の文だけ覚えていた可能性があり、"了" の知識に関してはほぼなかったと考えられる。事後テストは .81（了 1 = .92, 了 2 = .62）で、遅延事後テストでは .79（了 1 = .90, 了 2 = .65）であった。事前テストについては、正答率がほぼゼロに近かったため、α 係数は計算されなかった。

表 4. 和文中訳テストの結果

	事前		事後		遅延事後	
	M	SD	M	SD	M	SD
合計（了1＋了2）						
了 1 群	0.89	3.28	53.13	28.39	69.20	23.19
了 2 群	0.00	0.00	68.50	33.10	72.50	34.61
了 1						
了 1 群	0.89	4.72	47.32	44.27	62.50	40.54
了 2 群	0.00	0.00	77.00	38.13	74.00	41.76
了 2						
了 1 群	0.89	4.72	58.93	28.23	75.89	24.98
了 2 群	0.00	0.00	60.00	36.80	71.00	35.85

注：灰色のセルが指導からテストまでの間隔を揃えた上での比較対象となっている。

　意味解釈テストの時と同様に、指導からテストまでの間隔を揃えた上で、両群のテスト結果を統計的に比較する。まず、"了 1" の得点に関しては、「了 1 群」の事後テストが 47.32% で、「了 2 群」の遅延事後テストが 74.00% であった。対応なしの t 検定の結果、「了 2 群」の方が「了 1 群」よりも統計的に有意に "了 1" の点数が高かった、$U = 229, p = .02, r = .32$。両群の得点の差の大きさを表す「効果量 ($r$)」は、.32 で小と中の間であった（Plonsky & Oswald, 2014）。一方、"了 2" の得点に関しては、「了 1 群」の遅延事後テストが 75.89% で、「了 2 群」の事後テストが 60.00% であった。「了 1 群」と「了 2 群」の間に統計的に有意な差はなかった、$U = 272, p = .14, r = .20$。しかし、「了 1 群」の方が「了 2 群」の点数よりも高く、効果量 (r) は、"了 1" の得点の差と大きく変わらず、.20 であった。以上の結果をまとめると、"了 1" の得点に関しては、「了 1 群」＜「了 2 群」

であったが、"了2"の得点に関しては、「了1群」＞「了2群」となる。

5. 考察

本研究の結果から、"了1"と"了2"の指導順序を変えることで、それぞれの習得に影響を与えることが示された。具体的には、産出的知識を測る和文中訳テストの結果から、"了1"の使用に関しては、「了2群」の方が「了1群」よりも正確に使うことができるようになり、"了2"の使用に関しては、「了1群」の方が「了2群」よりも正確に使うことができるようになった。しかし、受容的知識を測る意味解釈テストにおいては、両群に有意な差は見られなかった。このことは、受容的知識の方が、産出的知識よりも先に身につけることができやすく（Leow, 2015）、負荷の低い方のテストでは差が見られなかったからかもしれない。指導順序を変えたことの影響は、特に産出的知識において現れることが伺える。

今回のパイロット実験の結果から、日本語母語話者にとっては、"了2"の方が"了1"よりも習得が難しいことが分かっていたが、難しい項目を先に教えると、簡単な項目を先に教えるよりも、両方の項目の習得が進むということは見られなかった（cf., Ryu & Shirai, 2011）。どちらか一方の指導順序が総じて習得を促進するという結果にならなかった理由の一つとして、"了1"と"了2"の文法難易度を簡単に決めることができないことがある。漢字の形態的な類似度からの転移を考えると、"了1"のほうが簡単であるし、それをパイロット実験結果も支持していた。しかし、語順規則の難易度から見れば、"了2"の方がシンプルであり、習得が容易な側面もある。このような複数の側面から、"了1"と"了2"は文法難易度が異なるため、指導順序は様々なレベルで影響を与えているのかもしれない。

和文中訳テストの結果から、最初に教えた文法項目よりも、後に教えた項目の方が、習得が進んでいるということが読み取れる。その理由の1つとしては、2つ目に教えられた項目の方が、1つ目に学んだ"了"と比較をしながら、学ぶことができるため、記憶に定着しやすいということが考えられる。言い換えるならば、学習者は新しい"了"を、既有知識であるもう一方の"了"と比較しながら、自分の知識の中に取り込むことがしやすかった可能性が示唆された(Kupferborg & Olshtain, 1996)。また、本結果は、山崎（2010）が述べている「"了2"→"了1"」のほうが習得しやすいという主張とは異なっている。今回の和文中訳テストの結果から、"了1"から先に教えることと"了2"から先に教えることのどちらか一方だけが総じて良いということではないのかもしれない。ただし、今回の結果を、実際の大学における中国語教育に直接適用するには注意が必要である。一つの理由として、今回の実験では3週間にわたって、それぞれの"了"の指導を行ったが、それに比べて、実際の教科書では"了"に関して、与えられる例文の数や練習量は少ないと考えられる。そのため、「練習量」がより少ない場合（またはより多い場合）でも、今回の結果と同じになるのか、それとも練習量が変

わることで、提示順序の影響が大きくなるのかは、今後の研究で追試されて初めて分かることになる。

　今回の結果において、1つ興味深い傾向が見られた。それは、"了1"と"了2"の問題の得点に大きな差が見られなかったことである。パイロット実験では、"了2"の方が"了1"よりも難易度が高いということが推定されたが、本実験の事後テストと遅延事後テストの得点では、ほとんど両者に差が認められなかった。これは、本実験の実験参加者は、短期間の間に"了1"と"了2"を集中的に指導されて学習した結果、"了1"と"了2"の習得度に差が見られなかった可能性がある。日本人中国語学習者にとって、"了2"の習得が難しい理由の1つとして、「完了」の"了1"と比較して、「変化」を表すために"了2"を使わなくてはならないということ自体を思い出すことの難しさがある。パイロット実験の学習者は、テストを受けた時、直前に"了1"と"了2"を学習したわけではないため、"了2"の点数が低く、本実験の学習者のようにテストの前に集中して"了1"と"了2"の練習が行われている場合は、差が見られなくなったのかもしれない。また、この問題は今後の課題になるが、本実験の遅延事後テストよりも更に4週間後などにテストを行った場合は、結果が変わった可能性も考えられる（たとえば、「了1群」と「了2群」の間により顕著な差が出るなど）。

　本研究の分析では、指導とテストの間隔を統制した上で、"了"の指導順序の効果を検証した。しかし、そのような統制を行わずに、最終結果である遅延事後テストの結果を比べることで、より実際の教育において、指導順序を変えることで、どのくらいの差が生まれるかを調べることもできる。意味解釈テストの合計点を見てみると、「了1群」が75.11％で、「了2群」は81.25％であり、ほとんど差は見られなかった。同様に、和文中訳テストの遅延事後テストの結果においても、「了1群」（69.20％）と「了2群」（72.50％）の間には差はなかった。そのため、教育的な視点から見ても、指導順序を変えることの影響は、さして大きくない可能性があると考察できるであろう。

6. まとめ

　本研究では、パイロット実験で日本語母語話者にとって、"了2"の方が"了1"よりも習得が難しいということを示した。そして、本実験では、文法習得難易度の異なる"了1"と"了2"の指導順序を、実際の大学の教室で変えることで、それぞれの習得にどのような影響を与えるか調査した。結果、受容的知識に関しては、指導順序を変えても、習得には大きな影響が見られなかった一方、産出的知識に関しては、後に教えられた"了"の方が、習得が高まる結果が示唆された。表層的には同じ形式である"了"の2つの用法の指導順序を変えても、様々な要因が習得に影響し、"了1"と"了2"の指導順序が与える影響というのは現段階では限定的であると考えられる。今後は、他の文法項目などでも、指導順序に関する研究が更に行われることが必要だろう。

参考文献

秋葉多佳子・堀江薫・白井恭弘（2010）．「格助詞の学習・指導における投射モデルの応用」南雅彦（編）『言語学と日本語教育 VI』(pp. 29-45) 東京：くろしお出版．

荒川清秀（2010）．「"了"をいかに教えるか」『中国語教育』8:1-17.

木村英樹（1997）．「動詞接尾辞"了"の意味と表現機能」『大河内康憲教授退官記念中国語学論文集』(pp. 157-179) 東京：東方書店．

木村英樹（2012）．『中国語文法の意味とかたち』東京：白帝社．

白井恭弘（2002）．「第二言語における文法習得研究とその教育的示唆：解説（第1章　文法形式と機能の習得と使用）」日本言語文化学研究会増刊特集号編集委員会（編）『言語文化と日本語教育．増刊特集号、第二言語習得・教育の研究最前線』(pp. 20-27) 東京：凡人社．

山崎直樹（2010）．「"了"の導入—教科書における提示法の検討」『中国語教育』8: 67-79.

郭春貴（2010）．「"了"的病句傾向—日本学習者常见的错误」『中国語教育』8: 39-45.

刘月华・潘文娱・故桦（2001）．『实用现代汉语语法（增订本）』北京：商务印书馆．

吕叔湘编（1999）．『现代汉语八百词（增订本）』北京：商务印书馆．

王振宇（2014）．「关于"了"的习得情况调查和教学策略」『中国語教育』12: 69-88.

Andersen, R. W. (1984). The one to one principle of interlanguage construction. *Language Learning, 34*(4), 77-95.

Clark, E. V. (1987). The principle of contrast: A constraint on language acquisition. In B. MacWhinney (Ed.), *Mechanisms of language acquisition* (pp. 1-33). Hillsdale, NJ: Erlbaum.

Eckman, F. R., Bell, L., & Nelson, D. (1988). On the generalization of relative clause instruction in the acquisition of English as a second language. *Applied linguistics, 9*(1), 1-20.

Ishida, M. (2004). Effects of recasts on the acquisition of the aspectual form -te i-(ru) by learners of Japanese as a foreign language. *Language Learning, 54*(2), 311-394.

Kupferborg, I. & Olshtain, E. (1996). Explicit contrastive instruction facilitates the acquisition of difficult L2 forms. *Language Awareness, 5*(3-4), 149-165. doi:10.1080/09658416.1996.9959904

Lee, E. & Kim, H. Y. (2007). On crosslinguistic variations in imperfective aspect: The case of L2 Korean. *Language Learning, 57*(4), 651-685.

Leow, R. P. (2015). *Explicit learning in the L2 classroom.* New York, NY: Routledge.

Plonsky, L. & Oswald, F. L. (2014). How big is "big"? Interpreting effect sizes in L2 research. *Language Learning, 64*(4), 878-912. doi:10.1111/lang.

12079
Ryu, J. Y. & Shirai, Y. (2011). The effect of instructional order on the L2 acquisition of the Korean imperfective aspect. In G. Granena et al. (Eds.), *Selected Proceedings of the 2010 Second Language Research Forum* (pp. 158–168). Somerville, MA: Cascadilla Proceedings Project.

Yalçın, Ş. & Spada, N. (2016). Language aptitude and grammatical difficulty. *Studies in Second Language Acquisition, 38*(2), 239–263. doi:10.1017/S0272263115000509

Zobl, H. (1983). Markedness and the projection problem. *Language Learning, 33*(3), 293–313.

Zobl, H. (1985). Grammars in search of input and intake. In S. M. Gass & G. Madden (Eds.), *Input in second language acquisition* (pp. 329–344). Rowley, MA: Newbury House.

An empirical study on the effects of second language grammar instruction: Comparison of Chinese verbal *-le* and sentential *-le*

Tingjie XU, Oita Prefectural College of Arts and Culture
Yuichi SUZUKI, Kanagawa University
Biao LIU, Kyushu University

Abstract

The present study examined whether the order of instruction of two grammatical structures that share the same surface (phonological and orthographical) form in Chinese ('verbal *-le*' [*le1*] and 'sentential *-le*' [*le2*]) influenced second language (L2) outcomes. Beginner-level Chinese L2 learners received explicit instruction on the two structures in a classroom setting. Two experimental groups received the same instructional contents, but the order of *le1* and *le2* instruction was reversed: (a) teaching *le1* followed by *le2* (*le1* group) or (b) teaching *le2* followed by *le1* (*le2* group). The results showed that the acquisition of *le2* was facilitated for the *le1* group, whereas the acquisition of *le1* was facilitated for the *le2* group, suggesting that manipulating the order of grammar instruction induced different learning processes.

付録1　完了の了「了1」の文法説明

　付録の中国語例文では日本語訳があるが、実際の授業資料では日本語訳はついていない。なお、授業資料では、中国語の例文に、発音を表す中国語のピンインをルビとしてつけているが、ここでは、スペースの制約上、ピンインなしで示している。

1. 以下の3つの文を見て、日本語でどんな意味かを考えよう。

　① 我学习6个月汉语。（学习汉语、6个月）
　　（私は中国語を6か月勉強する。）
　② 我买1件衣服。（买衣服、1件）
　　（私は服を一着買う。）
　③ 我 借 1 本 书。（借书、1本）
　　（私は本を一冊借りる。）

2. 以下の文は、上記の1の文と比べて、意味・形式的にどう異なるかを観察してみよう。

　① 我 学习 了 6 个月 汉语。（学习汉语、6个月）
　　（私は中国語を6か月勉強した。）
　② 我 买 了 1 件 衣服。（买衣服、1件）
　　（私は服を一着買った。）
　③ 我 借 了 1 本 书。（借书、1本）
　　（私は本を一冊借りた。）

「完了の了」の用法のまとめ

時間表現	主語	動詞	了	数量表現	目的語
今年	我	学习	了	6个月	汉语
今年、私は中国語を6ヶ月勉強した。					
上个月	我	买	了	1件	衣服
先月、私は洋服を一着買った。					
上星期	我	借	了	1本	书
先週、私は本を一冊借りた。					

「完了の了」意味：動詞の後ろにつき、ある動作の完了を表す。
　　　　　　　　　（〜しました）
　　　　　　　　よく数量表現（例：1着の〜）とともに用いられる。

付録2　完了の了「了1」の練習

練習1：以下の日本語文を中国語に訳してみてください。

1. 今日、私は2つのおにぎりを食べた。（饭团、吃、2个、今天）
2. 昨日、彼女は3時間の運動をした。（做、运动、昨天、3小时、她）
3. 昨日、彼は2杯のビールを飲んだ。（啤酒、喝、2杯、他）
4. 昨日、彼女は2コマの授業を受けた。（上、课、2节）

練習2：以下の中国語を日本語に訳し、そして質問に答えてみよう。ペアの人とお互い、確認してみよう。

1. 上星期、你学了「多长时间」汉语？（どれぐらいの時間）
   （先週、あなたは中国語をどれぐらいの時間勉強した？）
   ・日本語の意味：＿＿＿＿＿＿＿＿＿＿＿＿＿＿＿＿＿＿＿＿
   ・答え：＿＿＿＿＿＿＿＿＿＿＿＿＿＿＿＿＿＿
2. 暑假、你买了几件衣服？（几、いくつ）
   （夏休み、あなたは服を何着買った？）
   ・日本語の意味：＿＿＿＿＿＿＿＿＿＿＿＿＿＿＿＿＿＿＿＿
   ・答え：＿＿＿＿＿＿＿＿＿＿＿＿＿＿＿＿＿＿
3. 昨天、你看了几个小时电视？（看电视、テレビを見る）
   （昨日、あなたはテレビを何時間見た？）
   ・日本語の意味：＿＿＿＿＿＿＿＿＿＿＿＿＿＿＿＿＿＿＿＿
   ・答え：＿＿＿＿＿＿＿＿＿＿＿＿＿＿＿＿＿＿
4. 昨天、你上了几节课？
   （昨日、あなたは授業を何コマ受けた？）
   ・日本語の意味：＿＿＿＿＿＿＿＿＿＿＿＿＿＿＿＿＿＿＿＿
   ・答え：＿＿＿＿＿＿＿＿＿＿＿＿＿＿＿＿＿＿
5. 上学期、你买了几本教科书？
   （先学期、あなたは教科書を何冊買った？）
   ・日本語の意味：＿＿＿＿＿＿＿＿＿＿＿＿＿＿＿＿＿＿＿＿
   ・答え：＿＿＿＿＿＿＿＿＿＿＿＿＿＿＿＿＿＿

付録3　完了の了「了1」の練習

「完了の了」
「完了を表す了」を使って絵の動作の完了したことを中国語で書きましょう。

1. 鸡蛋、个、买、晚上

夜、彼は10個の卵を買いました。
_____

2. 电视、小时、个、看、昨天晚上

昨夜、彼らは3時間テレビを見ました。
_____

3. 眼镜、副、买、星期一

月曜日、彼女は1つのメガネを買いました。
_____

4. 网球、下午、打、小时、个

午後、彼らは1時間テニスをしました。
_____

付録 4　変化の了「了 2」の文法説明

1. 以下の 4 つの文を見て、日本語でどんな意味かを考えよう。

　　① 我是大学生。（私は大学生だ。）
　　② 今天我不去图书馆。（今日私は図書館に行かない。）
　　③ 这件衣服很便宜。（便宜、安い）（この服、とても安い。）
　　④ 今天天气不冷。（天气、天気；冷、寒い）（今日の天気、寒くない。）

2. 以下の文は、上記の文と比べて、意味・形式的にどう異なるかを観察してみよう。

　　① 我是大学生了。（私は大学生になった）
　　② 今天我不去图书馆了。（今日私は図書館に行くのをやめた。）
　　③ 这件衣服便宜了。（この服、安くなった。）
　　④ 今天天气不冷了。（今日の天気、寒くなくなった。）

「変化の了」の用法のまとめ

主語	述語	目的語	了	構造
我	是	大学生	了	「是＋名詞＋了」
私は大学生になった。				
我	不去	图书馆	了	「不＋動詞＋了」
私は図書館に行くのをやめた。				
这件衣服	便宜		了	「形容詞＋了」
この洋服、安くなった。				
今天天气	不冷		了	「不＋形容詞＋了」
今日の天気、寒くなくなった。				

「変化の了」の意味：了を文末に置き、変化を表す（〜になった）。

付録5　変化の了「了2」の練習

練習1：以下の日本語文を中国に訳してみてください。

1. 私は成人になった。（成年人）
2. 私はお酒を飲まなくなった（喝酒）。
3. アイフォンが安くなった。（苹果手机、便宜）
4. ユニクロの洋服が安くなくなった。（优衣库的衣服、便宜）

練習2：過去と現在の変化について考えてみよう・言ってみよう。まず、それぞれの文の前半を日本語に訳し、その後、過去と比べ、現在はどうなっているかについて、中国語で言ってみよう。

1. 去年我是高中生（去年、私は高校生だ）、（日本語：　　　　　）
 今年（今年は）＿＿＿＿＿＿＿＿＿＿
2. 昨天这件衣服很贵（昨日、この服とても高かった）（日本語：　　）
 今天（今日は）＿＿＿＿＿＿＿＿＿＿
3. 以前我喝酒（以前、私はお酒を飲む）、（日本語：　　　　　　　）
 现在我（現在私は）＿＿＿＿＿＿＿＿＿＿
4. 汉语开始很难（中国語最初のころはとても難しい）、（日本語：　　）
 现在（現在は）＿＿＿＿＿＿＿＿＿＿
5. 昨天天气不冷（昨日の天気、寒くなかった）、（日本語：　　　　　）
 今天（今日は）＿＿＿＿＿＿＿＿＿＿

付録6　変化の了「了2」の練習

「変化の了」
「変化を表す了」を使って、絵の変化を説明しましょう。

1. 点、現在

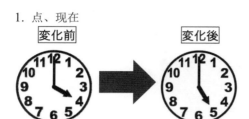

今、5時になりました。

2. 涼、面条

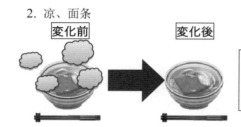

うどんが冷たくなりました。

3. 抽烟、不、他

彼は、たばこを吸わないことにしました。

4. 小张、苹果手机、买、不

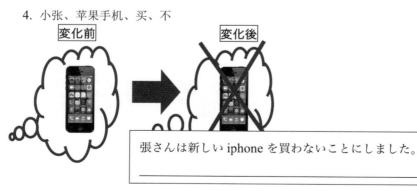

張さんは新しいiphoneを買わないことにしました。

Studies in Language Sciences
Journal of the Japanese Society for Language Sciences
Volumes 16 & 17, March 2018

編 者	言語科学会
発行者	武村哲司

2018 年 3 月 31 日　　第 1 版第 1 刷発行©

発行所　株式会社 開拓社	〒113-0023 東京都文京区向丘 1-5-2 電話 03-5842-8900（代表） 振替 00160-8-39587 http://www.kaitakusha.co.jp

印刷　日之出印刷株式会社　　　　　ISBN978-4-7589-1706-3 C3380